CLASSIC ROCK STORIES

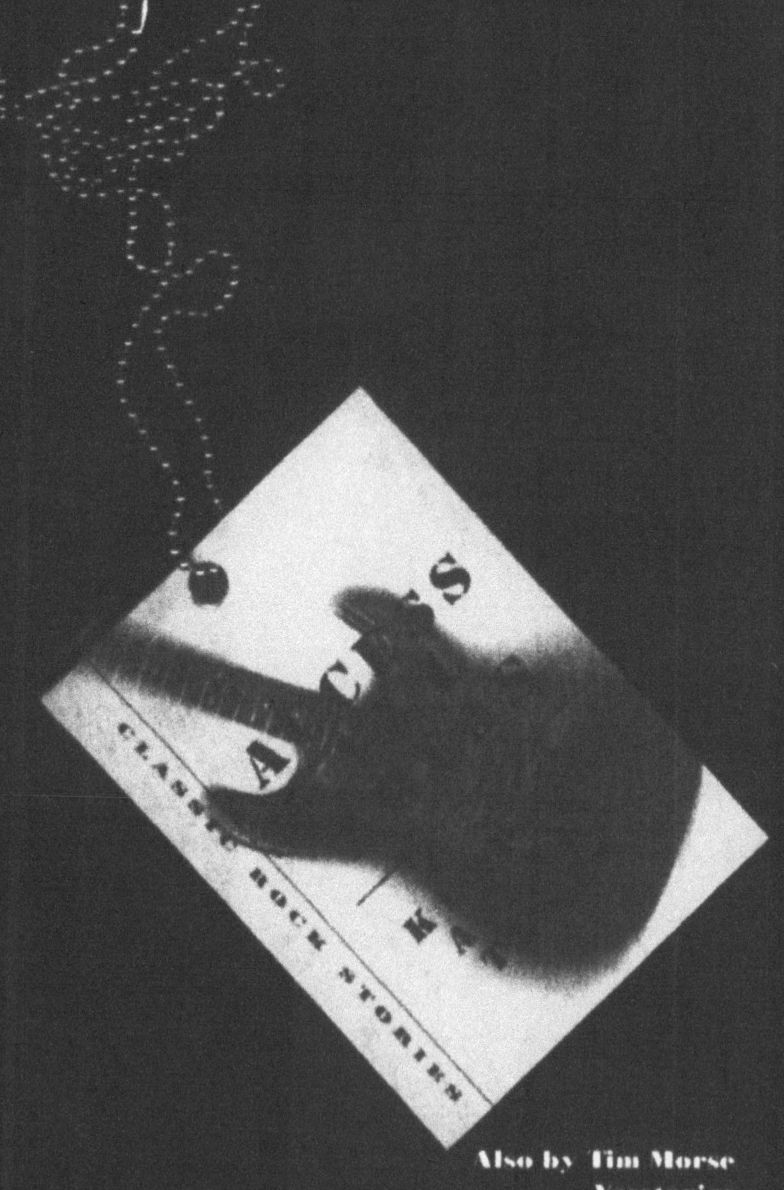

Also by Tim Morse

Yesstories

CLASSIC ROCK STORIES

The Stories Behind the Greatest Songs of All Time

TIM MORSE

St. Martin's Griffin • New York

 Printed in the United States of America. For information, address St. Martin's Press, 175 Fifth Avenue, New York, N.Y. 10010.

Design by Ellen R. Sasahara

Library of Congress Cataloging-in-Publication Data

Morse, Tim.
Classic rock stories / Tim Morse.
p. cm.
Includes bibliographical references and index.
ISBN : 978-0-312-18067-6
1. Rock music—History and criticism. 2. Rock musicians—Anecdotes. I. Title.
ML3534.M69 1998
781.66—dc21 98-14747
CIP
MN

D 25 27 29 30 28 26 24

Dedicated to Music Lovers Everywhere. . . .

Acknowledgments

I would like to thank the following people for letting me raid their archives for material used in this book: Tom Byrnes, Tony Finocchietti, Rich Martin, Larry Schweiger, and Rich Wilburn.

I am also gratefully indebted to the lovely Christine Holz for helping to set up interviews with some of the artists who appear in this book. She and Lisa Mikita run an excellent newsletter called the "Music News Network," which features many classic/progressive rock acts (for more information send a SASE to Music News Network, P.O. Box 21531, Tampa, FL 33622-1531). I also must thank Anne Leighton for her assistance in setting up interviews. Much appreciation is extended to the artists who agreed to be interviewed for this project: Ian Anderson, Peter Frampton, Chris Squire, and Martin Barre.

I would like to thank Pat Johnson and Mark Dean for their help in rounding up photos. Also appreciation must be expressed to Greg Cohn, my editor at St. Martin's Press, and his assistant Kim Walker for their help in making this project a reality. I am grateful for the excellent bed-and-breakfast service provided by Dick and Serene Clayton in Los Angeles (and for the B&B in the Bay area, owned and operated by Rich and Jennifer Martin). Lastly I must thank my friends and family for their support and love during the creation of this book.

Contents

Introduction

I was surrounded by music at a very young age, and I remember being thrilled by certain pop songs of the day in grade school. The first major rock influence in my life was the Beatles. In the 1960s there was no escaping the Beatles, and if you weren't alive then, you cannot really know what the mania was like for them. I distinctly remember my dad telling me that this was an important group as they performed "Hey Jude" on the David Frost show. I heard that song on the radio endlessly throughout that summer. I even recall my first-grade teacher playing one of their albums in class, but I don't know how she rationalized this at the time. I was nine years old when I got a guitar for Christmas, and my mission in life was to learn as many Beatle songs as possible.

By the time I was in middle school, I had friends exposing me to all sorts of different music: Led Zeppelin, Pink Floyd, Rick Wakeman, and Jethro Tull. I will never forget hearing the ominous opening notes of "Aqualung" for the first time and making the instant realization that this was music I hadn't experienced before. All of a sudden there was an explosion of exciting music, and musicians were encouraged to be individuals and to experiment with their art. In retrospect, I feel that this was the best era for rock music.

My first book was entitled *Yesstories* and was accordingly about the rock band Yes. Instead of focusing on the politics and personalities, I chose to direct my attention to the music the group had created. *Yesstories* was actually a biography of the music of Yes. So when that project was completed, it seemed to be a natural progression to take the same approach with classic rock as a genre. To do this it is important to get as many direct quotes from the songwriters themselves explaining how this music was created. As I started to put this project together

I realized that there wasn't any other book on classic rock that binded these stories in one volume, and it helped motivate me through hours and hours of research.

In a way there has never been a better time for classic rock. Classic rock radio stations have firmly established themselves in every major market in the United States. Currently a revival in the seventies and in classic rock is tuning people in to the classics. Many major bands from the era have re-formed to tour and write new music. It's interesting to note that five of the top ten touring acts of 1996 were classic rock bands (the Eagles, Kiss, Bob Seger, Rod Stewart, and Ozzy Osbourne). All of the songs featured in this book have come from platinum and gold albums—making the total in untold millions of albums represented. To discover the intriguing stories and secrets that formed the soundtrack of your life, just turn the page . . .

Tim Morse

Accidents Will Happen

Studio Incidents That Led to Award-Winning Songs

Life is full of happy accidents and coincidences. Sometimes while the composer/recording artist is almost an innocent bystander, a lucky series of them will fall into place and create a song that will become a classic on the radio.

SONG TITLE Mony Mony

ARTIST Tommy James and the Shondells

Featured on Anthology (repackage). Released 1990/Rhino (original release 1968)
Words & music by Bobby Bloom, Ritchie Cordell, Bo Gentry and Tommy James

Tommy James (singer/songwriter):

The night we wrote the song, we were absolutely devastated because we couldn't come up with a "Bony Moronie," a "Sloopy" kind of title, and we knew that's what it had to be. It had to be a girl's name that nobody had ever heard of before. We were going through the dictionary, but nothing was happening. We were just absolutely frustrated. I walked out onto my terrace—I lived in Manhattan at the time—and I'm just sort of scanning around and I'm looking for just any part of a name, anything. I'm just kind of staring out into space, and all of a sudden, I look up and I see . . . I said [to my manager], "Ritchie, c'mere." He came over and I said, "Look." And all of a sudden, here's this M.O.N.Y. with a dollar sign in the middle of the "O." [The sign was for the Mutual of New York Insurance Company!] The song kind of etched in stone in New York. We both just fell down laughing.

SONG TITLE **Dust in the Wind**

ARTIST **Kansas**

Featured on Point of Know Return. Released 1977/Kirshner
Words & music by Kerry Livgren

Kerry Livgren (songwriter/guitarist):

A lot of people seem to identify with what I said in that song. And that really surprised me, because in a way it's kind of a dismal song. I was reading a book of American Indian poetry when I came across that line—this American Indian said, "For all we are is dust in the wind." And I thought, "You know, that's really true. I've got all this success and material possessions and a goal in my life was accomplished at that point, but I am going back into the ground. And what does this really mean in light of that?" And that's kind of the message in that song. But the amazing thing was that so many people identified with it, and that song ended up on the country charts, middle of the road charts, easy listening . . . it crossed all kinds of boundaries.

I was always the lead guitar player in the band, a rock and roll electric guitar player, and I've never really been an acoustic guitar player. So I was trying to expand my musical horizons on the acoustic guitar by learning to fingerpick. So I made up this finger exercise to teach myself how to fingerpick. And I was sitting in my music room playing this thing, and my wife walked by and she stood there and listened and then said, "That's really pretty. You should make words to that." I said, "No, honey this is just something I'm trying to learn to do." And she said, "No, that's really nice. Don't forget that now." And she kept bugging me about this pretty thing, she really seemed to latch onto it. So I turned it into a song.

We were almost done with rehearsals for *Point of Know Return,* and we had pretty well learned all the songs. Someone said, "Have you got any more songs?" And I said, "Well . . . I've got this one, but you guys wouldn't like it. It's *not* Kansas. I'm really hesitant to even play it." And they insisted that I play it, and when I did it on the acoustic guitar the band agreed, "We need to be doing this song." And I was amazed; in fact, I rejected the idea. I actually fought with the band over the fact that we shouldn't do this song. "This is not us . . ." Well, it shows you what I know, because it turned out to be our biggest hit ever.

SONG TITLE Badge

ARTIST Cream

Featured on Goodbye. Released 1969/Polydor
Words & music by Eric Clapton and George Harrison

George Harrison (singer/songwriter/guitarist):

That whole song was quite silly. Ringo was sitting around drinking, out of his brain, saying anything. The part about "Our kid, now he's married to Mabel," well, "our kid" is a common Liverpool expression that usually means your younger brother. We were amusing ourselves.

Ringo came in—he was absolutely plastered and we were up to the lines: "I told you not to drive in the dark/ I told you . . ." And Ringo said, "About the swans that live in the park!"

SONG TITLE **Boris the Spider**

ARTIST the Who

Featured on A Quick One (Happy Jack). Released 1966/MCA
Words & music by John Entwistle

John Entwistle (songwriter/bassist):

I just had a childhood fear of spiders. In England they always seem to be on the ceiling—always up there. I just described a spider sort of crawling down, and then you squash it, that sort of thing. I don't like name-dropping, but I was sitting next to Bill Wyman one night down at the club, and we started talking about spiders, and I thought of a name for a spider: Boris the spider. Our production manager, the fellow with the bald head, he was driving my Bentley, he said, "That would be a good title for a song 'Boris the Spider.' " I had been contracted to write two numbers on the Who LP by the publisher who had given me an advance, and I'd already written "Whiskey Man," and I had to write another one for the album. And, like, we were recording it at the time. So I thought I might as well settle that and write another one about a spider called Boris. And we stayed up half the night, and I said to him, "How about a chorus going 'creepy, creepy, crawly, crawly'?" I mean I just sort of wrote the words, and the next morning I got up at ten and did the demo tape of it. That was just the amount of thought that went into it. It was like a drunken booze-up. We just did it as a joke.

SONG TITLE **Friend of the Devil**

ARTIST the Grateful Dead

Featured on American Beauty. Released 1970/Warner Brothers
Words & music by Robert Hunter and Jerry Garcia

Robert Hunter (lyricist):

I was playing bass for the New Riders of the Purple Sage, although I never actually got to the stage with them. We were sitting around practicing one night, and I had "Friend of the Devil" more or less written. I said, "Try this out," and then David Nelson and John Dawson helped work out the changes. I still have the recording of that evening, and it's not that different. We went down to get some coffee, and Marmaduke [Dawson] said, "It's real good, but it has that one repeating line, 'It looks like water but it tastes like wine.' Can you get anything punchier?" So I said, "I've got it. How about, 'A friend of the devil is a friend of mine?' " He said, "You got it. That's it!" So I took the tape with me back to the house where we were staying, and when I got up the next morning, I heard [Jerry] Garcia listening to the tape, with that funny look in his eye. The next thing you know he'd written a bridge for it. He wrote the "Anne Marie" part. Before that it was the same melody all the way through. Then the Grateful Dead snatched it up, much to the New Riders' dismay.

SONG TITLE Substitute

ARTIST the Who

Featured on Meaty, Beaty, Big & Bouncy. Released 1971/MCA
Words & music by Peter Townshend

Peter Townshend (singer/songwriter/guitarist):

It was written as a spoof on "Nineteenth Nervous Breakdown." On the demo I sang with an affected Jagger-like accent, which Kit obviously liked, as he suggested the song as a follow-up to "My Generation." The lyric has come to be the most quoted Who lyric ever. It somehow goes to show that "trust the art, not the artist" tag that people put on Dylan's silence about his work could be a good idea. To me, "Mighty Quinn" is about the five Perfect Masters of the age, the best of all being Meher Baba of course, to Dylan it's probably about gardening, or the joys of placing dog shit in the garbage to foul up Alan J. Weberman. "Substitute" makes me recall writing a song to fit a clever and rhythmic-sounding title. A play on words. Again it could mean a lot more to me now than it did when I wrote it. If I told you what it meant to me now, you'd think I take myself too seriously.

The stock, downbeat riff used in the verses, I pinched from a record played to me in "Blind Date," a feature in *Melody Maker*. It was by a group who later wrote to thank me for saying nice things about their record in the feature. The article is set up so that pop stars hear other people's records without knowing who they are by. They say terrible things about their best mates' latest, and it all makes the pop scene snottier and more competitive. Great. The record I said nice things about wasn't a hit, despite an electrifying riff. I pinched it, we did it, you bought it.

SONG TITLE While My Guitar Gently Weeps

ARTIST the Beatles

Featured on The Beatles ("the White Album"). Released 1968/Capitol
Words & music by George Harrison

George Harrison (singer/songwriter/guitarist):

I had a copy of the *I Ching—The Book of Changes,* which seemed to me to be based on the Eastern concept that everything is *relative to* everything else, as opposed to the Western view that things are merely coincidental.

This idea was in my head when I visited my parents' house in the north of England. I decided to write a song based on the first thing I saw upon opening any book—as it would be *relative* to that moment, at that time. I picked up a book at random, opened it—saw "gently weeps"—then laid the book down again and started the song. Some of the words to the song were changed before I finally recorded it.

When we actually started recording "While My Guitar . . ." it was just me playing the acoustic guitar and singing it, and nobody was interested. Well, Ringo probably was, but John and Paul weren't. When I went home that night I was really disappointed, because I thought, "Well, this is really quite a good song; it's not as if it's crap!" And the next day I happened to drive back into London with Eric [Clapton], and while we were in the car I suddenly said, "Why don't you come and play on this track?" And he said, "Oh, I couldn't do that, the others wouldn't like it," . . . So Eric was reluctant and I finally said, "Well, damn, it's my song and I'd like you to come down," . . . [And] everybody started behaving and not fooling around so much! And the song came together nicely.

SONG TITLE Bouree

ARTIST Jethro Tull

Featured on Stand Up. Released 1969/Chrysalis
Music by J.S. Bach (arrangement by Ian Anderson/Jethro Tull)

Ian Anderson (singer/songwriter/instrumentalist):

I was fortunate enough to hear "Bouree" daily through the floor of my apartment, because a music student was busy practicing on his classical guitar downstairs from me. So "Bouree" was kind of stuck in my brain when I was looking for an instrumental piece to play in 1969. We had quite a lot of different arrangements of that piece, but I don't necessarily remember exactly where it all fits in, especially since some of it is, shall we say, improvisation.

SONG TITLE Sympathy For the Devil

ARTIST the Rolling Stones

Featured on Let It Bleed. Released 1969/ABKCO
Words & music by Mick Jagger and Keith Richards

Keith Richards (guitarist/songwriter):

It started as sort of a folk song with acoustics, and ended up as a kind of mad samba, with me playing bass and overdubbing the guitar later. That's why I don't like to go into the studio with all the songs worked out and planned beforehand. Because you can write the songs, but you've got to give the band something to use its imagination on as well. That can make a very ordinary song suddenly come alive into something totally different, just because they're not being dictated to, "No you've got to play this, because this is how the song goes," Charlie [Watts] will say, "It feels more like this," and suddenly it's a totally different song . . . You can write down the notes that are being played, but the thing that you can't put down is the "Factor X"—which is so important in rock and roll—which is the feel.

SONG TITLE **Fame**

ARTIST **David Bowie**

Featured on Young Americans. Released 1975/Rykodisc (rerelease)
Words & music by David Bowie, John Lennon and Carlos Alomar

David Bowie (singer/songwriter):

My band had been working onstage with an old single by the Flares called "Foot Stompin'." The riff that Carlos [Alomar] had developed for it I found fascinating. I kept telling him that it was a waste to do it on somebody else's song, and that we should use that on something of our own. So we were playing that riff for John Lennon in the studio—he came down for the day—and we said, "What do you make of this, John?" He was playing along with it, just muttering to himself in a corner, saying, "—aim!—aim!" It just all fell into place when he said, "Fame!"

We said, "That's great, John! Hey, John, help us write this song called 'Fame'!" John carried on playing the rhythm guitar, and we just put the whole backing track together in about 15 to 20 minutes. It was a real "Hey-let's-do-the-show-right-here" Mickey Rooney thing. Then I took the idea of fame and just ran away and wrote the lyrics for it. The next day John came down again and said "Hey, that's real good, that one!"

SONG TITLE **Hocus Pocus**

ARTIST **Focus**

Featured on Moving Waves. Released 1971/IRS
Music by Thijs Van Leer and Jan Akkerman

Thijs Van Leer (singer/songwriter/instrumentalist):

We were all sitting around the recording studio when Pierre began to play two-bar drum fills. Jan answered him on the guitar with a light-hearted tune. I didn't want to be outdone, and for the first time in my life I yodeled. Everyone considered it a very funny joke, but we found ourselves drawn back to the song.

SONG TITLE **Lucky Man**

ARTIST Emerson, Lake and Palmer

Featured on Emerson, Lake and Palmer. Released 1970/Atlantic
Words & music by Greg Lake

Greg Lake (singer/songwriter/bassist):

I actually wrote that when I was 12 years old. During the making of the first album, we ran out of material; it came to the end of the record, and we were one song short. There were vacant looks across the studio—"Does anybody have any more ideas?"—and terribly glum faces everywhere. I said, "I've got this folk tune that I wrote on acoustic guitar when I was a kid." Everyone said, "Oh, go on then, let's hear it." I strummed it out, and the reaction was, "Yeah, a cup of tea . . ." Total disinterest. But we had to have something, so we decided to try and record it. Carl and I went out into the room with just a Gibson J-200 acoustic guitar, drums, and voice; I sang and he played along—and it sounded like shit! Then I put the bass guitar on it, and soon as I did that, it sounded more like a complete thing.

Keith said, "Let's see what I can do with it," and he started fooling around with a Moog synthesizer, rehearsing away, playing along with the whole track. Halfway through, I kind of liked what he was playing, so I put the machine into record.

Keith Emerson (songwriter/keyboardist):

I improvised something. I didn't think much of the solo. Honestly, it's a lot of shit. But it was just what he wanted. I just did a rough setting on the synthesizer, went in, and played something off the top of my head.

SONG TITLE **Question**

ARTIST the Moody Blues

Featured on Question of Balance. Released 1970/Polydor
Words & music by Justin Hayward

Justin Hayward (singer/songwriter/guitarist):

This would have to be my number one favorite, because it is so very different. . . . It was originally two songs. I was under pressure on a Friday night—I knew we had three hours of studio time booked for the next day—and I was expected to turn up with a song that still wasn't finished. So I just put two songs together and strung the lyrics together to make it work—and it worked! The two had always been in the same key and the same tuning, but because of the different tempos I'd never thought of putting them together.

SONG TITLE **Paint It Black**

ARTIST the Rolling Stones

Featured on Aftermath. Released 1966/ABKCO
Words & music by Mick Jagger and Keith Richards

Keith Richards (songwriter/guitarist):

Mick wrote it. I wrote the music, he did the words. Get a single together. What's amazing about that one for me is the sitar. Also, the fact that we cut it as a comedy track. Bill was playing an organ, doing a take-off of our first manager, who started his career in show business as an organist in a cinema pit. We'd been doing it with funky rhythms and it hadn't worked, and he started playing like this and everybody got behind it. It's a two-beat—very strange. Brian playing sitar makes it a whole other thing.

SONG TITLE Sweet Emotion

ARTIST Aerosmith

Featured on Toys in the Attic. Released 1975/Columbia
Words & music by Steven Tyler and Tom Hamilton

Tom Hamilton (bassist/songwriter):

I wrote that line on bass and realized I should think of some guitar parts for it if I was ever going to get a chance to present it to the band. I didn't think I ever would. But it was at the end of the recording, and Jack said, "Tomorrow's jam day, if anybody's got a stray riff hanging around." I said, "Yeah, I do." So I spent the day showing everybody everything, and we took it from there, refining it into what it is. Steven had the idea of taking that intro riff, which became the chorus bass line under the "sweet emotion" part, and transposing it into the key of E, and making it a really heavy Zepplinesque thing.

Steven Tyler (singer/songwriter):

We didn't know how to end it . . . we got into a big fight. Blew [cocaine] all over the place. It was late, and we were at the end of our rope. Finally I said, "Just fuckin' play a drum fill, and we'll go into [sings outro riff]." And we did it. It was such a magic moment.

A lot of stuff I wrote in the old days just came out of anger. "Sweet Emotion" was about how pissed off I was at Joe's ex-wife, and all the other frustrations of the time. I could never get through to him.

SONG TITLE **Tush**

ARTIST ZZ Top

Featured on Fandango! Released 1975/Warner Brothers
Words & music by Billy Gibbons, Dusty Hill and Frank Beard

Billy Gibbons (songwriter/guitarist):

That song came together one evening. The particular room we were playing in was about 100 percent and was one of those nights where nobody wanted to quit. We kept on playing and just started making it up, and that tune literally came out as we went along. Dusty made up the words, and it kind of stuck. We kept using it. That particular tune has become an old standard now.

SONG TITLE **Breakdown**

ARTIST Tom Petty and the Heartbreakers

Featured on Tom Petty & the Heartbreakers. Released 1976/Gone Gator
Words & music by Tom Petty

Tom Petty (singer/songwriter/guitarist):

I wrote "Breakdown" in the studio about 11 years ago, and the first version was seven minutes long, with this long guitar solo in the end. Everyone had gone home, and I was sitting there listening, and in walks [singer] Dwight Twilley. Right in the fade-out of the song, Campbell plays [sings the song's melodic hook]. Twilley turns to me and says, "That's the lick, man! How come he only plays it once at the end of the song? It's the whole hook." I listened back, and he was right. So I called the band up—four in the morning—and told them to come back down. We did it again around the lick, took a couple of takes, and there it was.

SONG TITLE **Fanfare for the Common Man**

ARTIST Emerson, Lake and Palmer

Featured on Works Vol. 1. Released 1977/Atlantic
Music by Aaron Copland (arrangement by Emerson, Lake and Palmer)

Greg Lake (singer/songwriter):

Keith was playing it as a piece of classical music. I played this shuffle bass line behind him, and all of a sudden it started to connect. Then Carl came in the studio, and the three of us started to play it. Luckily enough, the engineer had a two-track running, and that is what's on the record—the first time we played through the piece.

SONG TITLE **You Ain't Seen Nothin' Yet**

ARTIST Bachman-Turner Overdrive

Featured on Not Fragile. Released 1974/Mercury
Words & music by Randy Bachman

Randy Bachman (singer/songwriter):

That song is a joke. A gold joke. I did the stuttering as a joke. If you met my brother Gary, you'd know he stutters. There was no intentional copy of "My Generation." I didn't even think of it at the time. All it was was a dummy vocal track. I wanted to make a cassette of the song and work on a solo over the weekend, so I laid down a funny vocal.

I took it home, and everybody laughed at it at first, but the engineer said, "You know, there's something really dynamite about that track. The b-b-baby is a hook." When we got back into the studio, I tried to do a straight vocal track. It sounded like Frank Sinatra singing "Strangers in the Night," so we all agreed to leave it on. Actually, I was kind of embarrassed by it. The Mercury people came down to Sound City in L.A., where I was mixing it, and when it came time for them to hear the song, I turned off the board.

SONG TITLE Magic Carpet Ride

ARTIST Steppenwolf

Featured on Steppenwolf the Second. Released 1973/MCA
Words & music by Moreve Rushton and John Kay

John Kay (singer/songwriter):

We were in the studio recording the second album, and Rushton came in, sat down with his bass, and said, "I wrote this song and it's really great." So we said, "Okay, play it," because everyone played their songs to the band. He played this three-chord pattern "Domp domp, da da da domp; domp domp da da da da domp domp" on his bass and sang, "I like my job, I like my baby." That was it . . . I had some ideas for it. I felt there wasn't enough to "I like my job." I took the tape home and put it on my new sound system. We were still living on Fountain Avenue, but it was after the first album so there was some money rolling in. One of the first things I had done with some of my royalties was to go down to the Sound Center and purchase my first real hi-fi system, brand-new. I had the system in the apartment for no more than a week, when I brought home this tape. Out came this "domp domp . . ." thing, and I just sort of let my mind flow. "I like to dream right between my sound machine"—the sound machine being the hi-fi system. Twenty minutes later the whole thing was finished.

SONG TITLE **Start Me Up**

ARTIST the Rolling Stones

Featured on Tattoo You. Released 1981/Virgin
Words & music by Mick Jagger and Keith Richards

Mick Jagger (singer/songwriter):

It was Keith's great riff, and I wrote the rest. The funny thing was that it turned into this reggae song after two takes. And that take on *Tattoo You* was the only take that was a complete rock and roll take. And then it went to reggae completely for about 20 takes, and that's why everyone said, "Oh, that's crap. We don't want to use that." And no one went back to Take 2, which was the one we used, the rock track.

Keith Richards (songwriter/guitarist):

That was in the can for ages, and mostly we'd forgotten about it. . . . So to us it was that interminable reggae track we did way back when.

SONG TITLE **Walk This Way**

ARTIST **Aerosmith**

Featured on Toys in the Attic. Released 1975/Columbia
Words & music by Steven Tyler and Joe Perry

Steven Tyler (singer/songwriter):

It started out as a Joe Perry guitar riff, and then I put my rhythmic lyrics that stem from my early days as a drummer on top. I remember making up those lyrics the night we were meant to record vocals. I wrote 'em on the walls of the Record Plant stairway.

Tom Hamilton (bassist/songwriter):

We were rehearsing that riff, and I don't think Steven was even around that day as we practiced it and arranged it. And that night we went with Jack Douglas to the movies and saw *Young Frankenstein.* There's that part in the movie where Igor says, "Walk this way," and the other guy walks the same way with the hump and everything. We thought it was the funniest thing we'd ever seen in our lives. So we told Steven the name of this song has got to be "Walk This Way," and he took it from there.

SONG TITLE **Benny and the Jets**

ARTIST Elton John

Featured on Goodbye Yellow Brick Road. Released 1973/MCA
Words & music by Elton John and Bernie Taupin

Elton John (singer/songwriter/pianist):

It's the strangest track on the whole album. It's a send-up of the glitter rock thing, and I sound like Frankie Valli of the Four Seasons.

I wanted "Candle in the Wind" to be the first single off the album, and I was recording *Caribou* at the time, it was when we were in Colorado and I still to this day can't see "Benny and the Jets" as a hit single, but a guy called Pat Pipolo from MCA Records rang me up and said, "You're Number One Black in Detroit," and I said, "I beg your pardon?" And he said, "It's the Number One Black record in Detroit." I said, "Black record—me in the R & B charts? Spit it out! Be it on your head if it isn't a hit," you know, like really considerate of me . . . sometimes an artist doesn't know what's good and what's bad, he knows what he feels about a track, but he doesn't know how to pick singles.

SONG TITLE **Black Water**

ARTIST the Doobie Brothers

Featured on What Were Once Vices Are Now Habits. Released 1974/Warner Brothers
Words & music by Pat Simmons

Ted Templeton (producer):

It shows you what great ears I have—I put "Black Water" on the B-side because I figured that's an acoustic thing. And all of a sudden a small station in South Carolina picked it up—that's when that sort of thing could happen, and then a big station picked it up. It became a number one record; it was forced out by radio.

SONG TITLE **Maggie May**

ARTIST **Rod Stewart**

Featured on Every Picture Tells a Story. Released 1971/Mercury
Words & music by Rod Stewart and Martin Quittenton

Rod Stewart (singer/songwriter):

"Maggie May" was an accident. It wasn't meant to go on the album. A mate of mine who I thought had good ears said, "Well, I don't think it's got much of a melody, and it's a bit long, you know?" I said, "Well, I only recorded ten tracks for this album. There's nothing left over, so it'll have to stay. I've run over budget."

Even more important is the fact that when it came out on a single, it was a B-side; "Reason to Believe" was the A-side. And it was a disc jockey in Cleveland, I believe, that turned it over. Otherwise, I wouldn't be here today. I'd still be digging graves in the cemetery.

SONG TITLE **Minute by Minute**

ARTIST **the Doobie Brothers**

Featured on Minute by Minute. Released 1978/Warner Brothers
Words & music by Michael McDonald

Michael McDonald (singer/songwriter):

The success of "Minute by Minute" was a shock. I played it for a friend who was a mutual friend of the band—a good friend—and the guy didn't pull any punches, you know? He said, "I don't think so . . . it just doesn't have it!"

SONG TITLE **Take the Money and Run**

ARTIST the Steve Miller Band

Featured on *Fly Like an Eagle*. Released 1976/Capitol
Words & music by Steve Miller

Steve Miller (singer/songwriter/guitarist):

It's a goofy tune, a Bonnie and Clyde thing. I sort of left that one up to the record company, and they said, "Stop that one . . . it's a hit single!!!" Like they always do. I gave up on singles a long time ago. I used to work real hard on what I thought would be real good singles, and then I'd watch them through the weeks on the charts and they'd look like they fell down the mail chute at the Empire State Building.

SONG TITLE **Help Me**

ARTIST Joni Mitchell

Featured on *Court & Spark*. Released 1974/Asylum
Words & music by Joni Mitchell

Joni Mitchell (singer/songwriter):

"Help Me" is a throwaway song, but it was a good radio record. My record companies always had a tendency to take my fastest songs on albums for singles, thinking they'd stand out because they did on the LPs. Meantime, I'd feel that the radio is crying for one of my ballads.

SONG TITLE Don't Eat the Yellow Snow

ARTIST Frank Zappa

Featured on Apostrophe. Released 1974/Barking Pumpkin (rerelease)
Words & music by Frank Zappa

Frank Zappa (singer/songwriter/guitarist):

[Its success] was an accident. A disc jockey in Pittsburgh on a station that had a policy of playing novelty records of the sixties received the album in the mail, listened to "Yellow Snow". . . and said, "My God, it's a modern-day novelty record" . . . put it on the station that was part of a chain. It instantly goes into the top 20, it's picked up on all the stations on the chain.

SONG TITLE Heat Wave

ARTIST Linda Ronstadt

Featured on Prisoner in Disguise. Released 1975/Asylum
Words & music by Edward Holland, Brian Holland and Lamont Dozier

Linda Ronstadt (singer/songwriter):

I've turned down so many hits, you wouldn't believe it, especially in the days when I really needed them too. "I Don't Know How to Love Him" was one; "Help Me Make It through the Night" was another. I even felt that way about "Heat Wave." I loved it when Martha Reeves sang it. I threw it into my show when we were playing bars, because it was something fun that people could get drunk and rowdy to. I never had any intention of making a record out of it, but David Geffen said, "You've got to record that, it's a hit," and at that point, I realized that if I went ahead and did it, it would be good for me to have a hit. It would just make more sense for me in the long run, because then I could do more music that I wanted to do. The more secure my position was, the more I would be able to influence the music with my own taste. I did "Heat Wave," and I'm still sorry, because I hate to sing it. I don't think I sing it well, I don't think the record was good, and I cringe when it comes on the radio. I'm not doing it in the show anymore, and people are going to be bitching at me.

CLAPTON, Eric
(Photo by Josef M. Astro)

SONG TITLE I Shot The Sheriff

ARTIST Eric Clapton

Featured on There's One in Every Crowd. Released 1975/Polydor
Words & music by Bob Marley

Eric Clapton (singer/songwriter/guitarist):

At the time I didn't think it should go on the album, let alone be a single. I didn't think it was fair to Bob Marley, and I thought we'd done it with too much of a white feel or something. Shows what I know.

The record came out and went up the charts, and shortly after that I got a phone call from Bob. I don't remember where I was, or exactly what the circumstances were, but we had a half-an-hour conversation on the phone. Again, half of which I understood and half of which I didn't [laughter]. And I kept asking him if it was a true story—did he really shoot the sheriff? What was it all about? He wouldn't really commit himself. He said some parts of it were true, but he wasn't going to say which parts.

Cocaine

Songs About or Written on Drugs

Before there was a Betty Ford Clinic there was sex, drugs, and rock and roll. In the sixties and seventies a rock band whose members weren't doing drugs was an exception. Nowadays, of course, we are all a lot wiser about the use of foreign substances. But back in 1972 . . .

SONG TITLE Casey Jones

ARTIST the Grateful Dead

Featured on Workingman's Dead. Released 1970/Warner Brothers
Words & music by Robert Hunter and Jerry Garcia

Robert Hunter (lyricist):

I had just written down a line in my pocketbook that went, "Drivin' that train, high on cocaine, Casey Jones you'd better watch your speed." I thought it was very, very funny. I didn't think of it as a song or anything else, and I went on writing other songs. Then sometime later I went back to it and said, "Looks like there might be a song here." We were working it out, playing it for Stills and Crosby, jamming on it. Then when we decided to record it, I remember we discussed the word "cocaine," this being the time when that was still considered a very risky word, as was "God damn" on "Uncle John's Band." I said, "Give me some time to think about it," and I tried to write other concepts. I wrote, "Driving that train, whipping that chain." No. "Lugging propane." No. I tried any way to get away from it, and there just wasn't one. It had to go; there was no other line for that song.

SONG TITLE Do You Feel Like We Do?

ARTIST Peter Frampton

Featured on Frampton Comes Alive! Released 1976/A&M
Words & music by Peter Frampton

Peter Frampton (singer/guitarist/songwriter):

We would jam between rehearsing—which is always the boring part . . . and I came up with that lick. And we taped it, and we played it back and set about arranging it. The night before I'd written these three chords and the chorus, that's all I had. And so I stuck that on it. Then I realized the song was basically about a hangover! "I woke this morning with a wineglass in my hand." That afternoon we ended up writing the party song of all party songs, because the crowd loves to sing it. The first time we did it live, it tore the place apart, before anybody had ever heard it. It took me awhile to realize that I'd written one of these anthematic songs; but until you've done it in front of an audience, you just don't know. Also by accident, I realized I'm singing a question to the audience—if you ask them a question, they're going to answer you!

SONG TITLE She Said, She Said

ARTIST the Beatles

Featured on Revolver. Released 1966/Capitol EMI
Words & music by John Lennon and Paul McCartney

John Lennon (singer/songwriter):

That was written after an acid trip in L.A. during a break in the Beatles' tour where we were having fun with the Byrds and lots of girls. Some from *Playboy*, I believe. Peter Fonda came in when we were on acid, and he kept coming up to me and whispering, "I know what it's like to be dead."

He was describing an acid trip he'd been on. We didn't want to hear about that! We were on an acid trip and the sun was shining and the girls were dancing and the whole thing was beautiful and sixties, and this guy—who I really didn't know; he hadn't made *Easy Rider* or anything—kept coming over, wearing shades, saying, "I know what it's like to be dead," and we kept leaving him because he was so boring! And I used it for the song, but I changed it to "she" instead of "he."

SONG TITLE Katmandu

ARTIST Bob Seger

Featured on Beautiful Loser. Released 1975/Capitol
Words & music by Bob Seger

Bob Seger (singer/songwriter):

Katmandu is in Nepal. It's a city at the base of the Himalayan mountains. It's the highest city—elevation wise—in the world. They also smoke hash. It's legal there—one of the most godforsaken places on earth. It's a bit of a spoof on "Hey man, when is it goin' to happen for me, and if it doesn't, I'm getting out of here!"

SONG TITLE **Misty Mountain Hop**

ARTIST Led Zeppelin

Featured on Untitled (Led Zeppelin IV). Released 1971/Atlantic Records
Words & music by Robert Plant, Jimmy Page and John Paul Jones

Robert Plant (singer/songwriter):

It's about a bunch of hippies getting busted . . . about the problems you can come across when you have a simple walk in the park on a nice sunny afternoon. In England it's understandable, because wherever you go to enjoy yourself "Big Brother" is not far behind.

SONG TITLE **Doctor Wu**

ARTIST Steely Dan

Featured on Katy Lied. Released 1974/MCA Records
Words & music by Donald Fagen and Walter Becker

Donald Fagen (singer/songwriter):

"Doctor Wu" is about a triangle, kind of a love-dope triangle. I think usually when we do songs of a romantic nature, one or more of the participants in the alliance will come under the influence of someone else or some other way of life, and that will usually end up in either some sort of compromise or a split. In this song the girl meets somebody who leads another kind of life, and she's attracted to it. Then she comes under the domination of someone else, and that results in the ending of the relationship or some amending of the relationship. In "Doctor Wu" that someone else is a dope habit, personified as Doctor Wu.

SONG TITLE **Band on the Run**

ARTIST **Wings**

Featured on Band on the Run. Released 1973/Capitol EMI
Words & music by Paul McCartney

Paul McCartney (singer/songwriter/instrumentalist):

There were a lot of musicians at the time who'd come out of ordinary suburbs in the sixties and seventies and were getting busted. Bands like the Byrds, the Eagles—the mood amongst them was one of desperadoes. We were being outlawed for pot. It put us on the wrong side of the law. And our argument on the title song was, "Don't put us on the wrong side, you'll make us into criminals. We're *not* criminals, we don't want to be." We just would rather do this than hit the booze—which had been the traditional way to do it. We felt that this was a better move; we had all our theories.

So I just made up a story about people breaking out of prison. Structurally, that very tight little intro on "Band on the Run"—"Stuck inside these four walls"—led to a hole being blasted in the wall and we get the big orchestra and then we're off. We escape into the sun.

SONG TITLE **Good vibrations**

ARTIST the Beach Boys

Featured on Smiley Smile. Released 1967/Capitol
Words & music by Brian Wilson and Mike Love

Brian Wilson (singer/songwriter):

"Good Vibrations" was going to be the summation of my musical vision, a harmonic convergence of imagination and talent, production values and craft, songwriting and spirituality. I'd written it five months earlier and imagined the grand, Spector-like production while on the LSD trip I'd described so enthusiastically for Al. Instinctively, I knew it was the right song at the right time.

Written in three separate parts, "Good Vibrations" required seventeen sessions and six weeks—not six months as has always been reported—spread over three months, to record, costing a sum somewhere between $50,000 and $75,000, then an unheard amount for one song. I threw everything I could think of into the stew: fuzz bass, clarinet, cello, harp, and a theremin, a strange electronic instrument. Chuck Britz, who worked the board on all seventeen sessions, always said the first session was the best. Glen Campbell, one of the nearly twenty musicians used that day, agreed, exclaiming: "Whew, Brian! What were you smokin' when you wrote that?" A better question would've been, "What was I droppin'?"

SONG TITLE **Marrakesh Express**

ARTIST Crosby, Stills and Nash

Featured on Crosby, Stills and Nash. Released 1969/Atlantic
Words & music by Graham Nash

Graham Nash (singer/songwriter):

An actual journey I took in 1966 from Casablanca to Marrakesh, with my first wife Rose. I came back and played it for the Hollies, who rejected it, along with the first "Sleep Song." After a couple months of that, a man is liable to go insane, especially being the only one who was smoking grass at the time.

SONG TITLE White Punks on Dope

ARTIST the Tubes

Featured on The Tubes. Released 1975/A&M
Words & music by Bill Spooner, Roger Steer and Mike Evans

Bill Spooner (guitarist/songwriter):

It's about a bunch of rich kids we knew. You see all those ads on TV about drugs in the ghetto, and they say, "It's not their fault. They were born poor, and all they had to turn to was drugs." Well, in San Francisco, we know a whole bunch of these kids that are so rich, and they're all strung out, and they're total derelicts. So you don't have to be poor to be a derelict.

SONG TITLE Who Are You

ARTIST the Who

Featured on Who Are You. Released 1978/MCA
Words & music by Peter Townshend

Peter Townshend (singer/songwriter/guitarist):

I look back at my writing between 1972 and 1979, which is a period I was drinking a lot, and I don't see much growth. I can't remember when I recorded "Who Are You." Let me think. When I did the demo I was down at my studio in the country, and right, I remember, I was drunk when I did the backing vocals and I loved doing it, and a certain amount of that exhilaration has come through. But the song stands up as a song that was written in the cold light of a hangover following a rather nasty day. It's all academic. The song stands up or it doesn't stand up. And I'd like to think that where the song came from wasn't the fact that I was drunk when I did the demo, but the fact that I was fucking angry with Allen Klein, and that the song was an outlet for that anger. I'd like to think now that if I felt the same kind of anger again, I would be able to deal with it without needing to get drunk in order to smash my fist through a wall.

SONG TITLE Comfortably Numb

ARTIST Pink Floyd

Featured on The Wall. Released 1979/Columbia
Words & music by Roger Waters and David Gilmour

Roger Waters (singer/songwriter):

There's someone knocking at the door saying, "Come on, it's time to go." . . . So the idea is that they are coming to take him to the show because he's got to go perform that night, and they come into the room and realize something is wrong, and they actually physically bring the doctor in, and "Comfortably Numb" is about his confrontation with the doctor . . . because they're not interested in any of these problems. All they're interested in is how many people there are and tickets have been sold and the show must go on, at any cost, to anybody. I mean I personally have done gigs when I've been very depressed, but I've also done gigs when I've been extremely ill, where you wouldn't do any ordinary kind of work.

SONG TITLE **Back in the Saddle**

ARTIST **Aerosmith**

Featured on Rocks. Released 1976/Columbia
Words & music by Joe Perry and Steven Tyler

Joe Perry (guitarist/songwriter):

I was very high on heroin when I wrote "Back in the Saddle." That riff just floated right through me. Drugs can be a shortcut to creativity. All throughout history, medicine men and priests in all those primitive cultures used drugs to get to that spirit place. Ask any writer. You get to that place where your fingers are flying on the keyboard; you know the stuff is just flowing through you. But for a lot of writers, getting to that uninhibited place is difficult. So it's a shortcut just to have a beer. And it works for a while. But then you reach a point where it takes two beers to get there, then three. And after a while it's not working for you anymore, and your liver's going and the doctor is saying, "If you drink anymore, your nose is going to turn into a cauliflower." That's just us excessive bastards, you know. But with all drugs, you burn out on them, for different reasons. With heroin, your body just caves in. After a while all you care about is getting that buzz. Then you don't care about picking up a guitar. So it ends up blocking your creativity rather than helping it.

SONG TITLE **Delta**

ARTIST **Crosby, Stills and Nash**

Featured on Daylight Again. Released 1982/Atlantic
Words & music by David Crosby

David Crosby (singer/songwriter):

I had been fooling around with a phrase that had been in my head for some time; it had come from nowhere, as lyrics and phrases often do. I was telling it to Jackson Browne, who had come to visit with an expression on his face and a look in his eyes that meant worry—unexpressed, but palpable. To his credit, Jackson didn't dwell on it; he brought a strong, untainted energy with him, a pure creative force that's part of him. I mentioned the lines that had intrigued me. Jackson was excited and encouraging at the same time. They were embryonic lyrics, but he saw the promise in them or sensed the need in me to bring out more than was already there. He ragged me, got me to my feet, dragged my butt out of the house and into a car. He got me to Warren Zevon's house in Montecito, where there was a piano, and luckily for us, someone home. He sat me down at the piano, and once I got going he told me not to get up. I wanted to get up. I wanted to smoke my pipe, and my attention span at that time had the duration and constancy of a drunken butterfly's. But Jackson wouldn't let me up or let me at the pipe. He just stood there, looking over my shoulder, holding me at the bench, forcing me, slowly and painfully, to give birth to the song, not the lyrical fragment or the convenient phrase. The whole song. He kept me into it, threatened to break my arm if I got up (I outweighed him, but he's a wiry guy. Politically a pacifist, creatively he was an implacable fascist). It was an act of love and great caring; he showed concern for me, for my work, for seeing my work done. "Delta" was the last complete song that I wrote for years.

SONG TITLE The Needle and the Damage Done

ARTIST Neil Young

Featured on Harvest. Released 1972/Reprise
Words & music by Neil Young

Neil Young (singer/songwriter/guitarist):

I wrote that about Danny Whitten (guitarist for Crazy Horse). He'd gotten so wasted, so strung out, that he OD'ed and almost died . . . I never sat down with him and said, "Danny, listen to this." I don't believe that a song should be for one person. I just tried to make something that everyone could relate to.

SONG TITLE Heroin

ARTIST the Velvet Underground

Featured on The Velvet Underground & Nico. Released 1967/Verve
Words & music by Lou Reed

Lou Reed (singer/songwriter):

If someone's dumb enough to take heroin just because they heard my song, it's not my responsibility.

Meanwhile, Back in the Studio...

Inspiration in the Workplace

The recording studio can be a remarkably creative environment. Some artists have used it like a musical instrument (i.e. Pink Floyd) or had incredible, divinely inspired moments in the middle of a 12-hour session. Sometimes songs will be written or even assembled from different bits in the studio.

SONG TITLE **Bad Company**

ARTIST Bad Company

Featured on Bad Company. Released 1974/Swan Song
Words & music by Paul Rodgers and Simon Kirke

Paul Rodgers (singer/songwriter):

When I did the vocal for "Bad Company" . . . we put a microphone and headphones about a hundred yards out into this field in the dead of night, with just the moonlight to get an amazing atmosphere. So that's why there's quite a haunting sound to the voice. It was done in the middle of a field at the dead of night with the moon shining down . . . and we cut it in one take. It took about three hours to set it up, with wires and leads and everything, but when the time came there it was, and we just did it in the one take.

SONG TITLE **On the Border**

ARTIST the Eagles

Featured on On the Border. Released 1974/Asylum
Words & music by Don Henley, Glenn Frey and Bernie Leadon

Glenn Frey (singer/songwriter/guitarist):

We decided to get completely liberated on gin and tonics in order to do that little Temptations bit in the break. We had to be totally uninhibited where we didn't feel like we were going to sing the blues or anything, but like we were white, stoned punks, drunk out of our minds. We were just gonna go out there and have a good time!

SONG TITLE Black Dog

ARTIST Led Zeppelin

Featured on Untitled (Led Zeppelin IV). Released 1971/Swan Song
Words & music by Robert Plant, Jimmy Page and John Paul Jones

Jimmy Page (guitarist/songwriter):

We were always trying to encourage Jonesy [John Paul Jones] to come up with bits and pieces so to speak, 'cause that's usually what they were. He never came up with a complete whole song or anything, but he had this great riff with "Black Dog," and I added some sections to it as well . . . I suggested, how you get the breaks with the vocals. That's it, I've finally owned up, as no one else will in the band, but that was the idea to give it the vocal thing, then the riffs come in. I guess if you want to say that we leaned on something as far as the structure of it, you remember "Oh Well" by Fleetwood Mac, where it stops and there's a vocal, so there you are . . . now they'll sue us!

SONG TITLE One of These Nights

ARTIST the Eagles

Featured on One of These Nights. Released 1975/Asylum
Words & music by Glenn Frey and Don Henley

Don Felder (guitarist/songwriter):

Glenn [Frey] would go "One of these nights, cha cha chachacha cha cha chachacha," and that's it, no chord changes. Then I sat down and played bass on it and dubbed the bass part to it, and it was just me and Henley and Glenn sitting around and jamming. It's just being around, listening to ideas, criticizing ideas, and just working together.

NICKS, Stevie
(Photo by Pat Johnson Studios, S.F.)

SONG INFORMATION

SONG TITLE Gold Dust Woman

ARTIST Fleetwood Mac

Featured on Rumours. Released 1977/Reprise
Words & music by Stevie Nicks

Mick Fleetwood (drummer):

Stevie [Nicks] did her first vocal track of "Gold Dust Woman" in a fully lit studio. The song needed both a mysterious power and a lot of emotionality. As take followed take, Stevie began to withdraw into herself, reaching inside for the magic. The lights were dimmed; a chair was brought in so she could sit, saving her strength at three in the morning, and she wrapped herself in a big cardigan sweater to ward off the predawn chill. An hour later she was almost invisible in the shadows, elfin under big headphones, hunched over in her chair, alternately choosing from her supply of tissues, a Vicks inhaler, a box of lozenges for her sore throat, and a bottle of mineral water. Gradually she gained total command of her song. On the eighth take, exhausted but exalted, she sang the lyric straight through to perfection.

SONG TITLE Tumbling Dice

ARTIST the Rolling Stones

Featured on Exile on Main Street. Released 1972/Virgin
Words & music by Mick Jagger and Keith Richards

Andy Johns (producer):

That was a marathon tracking date. That went on for about two weeks. They would sit and play the intro riff over and over for hours and hours trying to get the groove right. We must have done 150 or 200 takes.

SONG TITLE Time

ARTIST Pink Floyd

Featured on Dark Side of the Moon. Released 1973/Capitol
Words & music by Roger Waters, David Gilmour, Rick Wright and Nick Mason

David Gilmour (singer/songwriter/guitarist):

Alan Parsons had just been sent out to do a recording in a clock shop for the sound effects library . . . and we were doing the song "Time," and he said, "Listen, I just did all these things, I did all these clocks," and so we wheeled out his tape and listened to it and said, "Great! Stick it on!"

SONG TITLE **Feels Like the First Time**

ARTIST Foreigner

Featured on Foreigner. Released 1977/Atlantic
Words & music by Mick Jones

Al Greenwood (keyboardist):

We started working on "Feels Like the First Time," and since we had a black drummer and disco was really in at the time, there was a lot of high-hat disco-type feel . . . if you listen to it now the chorus still has that open high hat. We started putting songs together and the bassist and drummer left—they thought it wasn't going anywhere!

SONG TITLE **Up on Cripple Creek**

ARTIST the Band

Featured on The Band. Released 1969/Capitol
Words & music by Robbie Robertson

Garth Hudson (keyboardist):

We would stick a wah-wah pedal on anything, and we tried it on the clavinet.

Levon Helm (drummer/singer):

There's a break in the music and Garth did that jaw harp thing and that was the hook that just pulled your ear right in.

SONG TITLE **You Can't Always Get What You Want**

ARTIST the Rolling Stones

Featured on Let It Bleed. Released 1969/ABKCO
Words & music by Mick Jagger and Keith Richards

Al Kooper (keyboardist):

Everyone sat around on the floor with either an acoustic guitar or a percussion instrument, and Mick and Keith played the song they wanted to record until everyone had the chord changes and the rhythm accents. There was a conga player who could play congas and roll huge hash joints without missing a lick. It was decided I would play piano on the basic track and overdub organ later.

I got into this groove I had on an Etta James record of "I Got You Babe" that really fit their song well. Keith picked up on it right away and played a nice guitar part that meshed right with it. When the proper take was gotten, Keith overdubbed an electric part and I overdubbed the organ.

SONG TITLE **Carry On**

ARTIST Crosby, Stills, Nash and Young

Featured on Déjà Vu. Released 1970/Atlantic
Words & music by Stephen Stills

Dallas Taylor (drummer):

The song was written in the middle of *Déjà Vu* sessions when Nash told Stephen they still didn't have an opener for the album. It was something of a message to the group, since it had become a real struggle to keep the band together at that point. Stephen combined two unfinished songs and stuck them onto a jam we'd had in the studio a few nights before, me on drums and Stephen on Hammond B-3.

SONG TITLE Echoes

ARTIST Pink Floyd

Featured on Meddle. Released 1971/Capitol
Words & music by Roger Waters, David Gilmour, Rick Wright and Nick Mason

Nick Mason (drummer):

We booked the studio for January, and throughout January we went in and played. Anytime that anyone had any sort of rough idea for something, we would put it down. It was a specific attempt to sort of do something by a slightly different method. By the end of January we listened back, and we'd got 36 different bits and pieces that sometimes cross related and sometimes didn't. "Echoes" was made up from that.

SONG TITLE Simple Man

ARTIST Lynyrd Skynyrd

Featured on (pronounced leh-nerd skin-nerd). Released 1973/MCA
Words & music by Gary Rossington and Ronnie Van Zant

Ed King (guitarist):

When we were just about done cutting the first album, we played "Simple Man" for [producer] Al Kooper, and he said, "You guys are *not* gonna record that song." So Ronnie took Kooper out to the parking lot, opened up the door to Kooper's Bentley, and said, "Get in." Kooper's sittin' there behind the wheel, and Ronnie shut the door and said, "When we're done cuttin' it, we'll call you." We cut the whole tune without him. When a band knows what it wants to do, it has to go with its heart and not listen to people on the outside.

SONG TITLE Friends

ARTIST Led Zeppelin

Featured on Led Zeppelin III. Released 1970/Swan Song
Words & music by Robert Plant and Jimmy Page

Jimmy Page (songwriter/guitarist):

Robert wrote the words. He did them all [on *Led Zeppelin III*] except on "Tangerine." The idea was to get an Indian style with the strings. The string players were not Indian, however, and we had to make some on-the-spot changes. John Paul Jones wrote an incredible string arrangement for this, and Robert shows his great range—incredibly high. He's got a lot of different sides to his voice which come across here. It has a menacing atmosphere. A friend came into the studio during the recording and it was bloody loud and he had to leave. He said, "You've really done something evil!"

SONG TITLE **Locomotive Breath**

ARTIST **Jethro Tull**

Featured on Aqualung. Released 1971/Chrysalis
Words & music by Ian Anderson

Ian Anderson (singer/songwriter/instrumentalist):

Songs like "Locomotive Breath" were very much contrived on the spot and very unsuccessfully in terms of trying to make the record . . . we just couldn't seem to get the thing to click at all. I was obviously not getting across how I wanted this song to sound to the other guys. It ended up with me sitting out in the studio—this was in the days before there were click tracks—I sat in the studio to be a click track for four and a half minutes by playing high hat and bass drum all the way through the track. Then I added some guitar parts, electric and acoustic guitar parts, and then tied into the front of that was John Evan's piano intro. Clive Bunker overdubbed the toms and the cymbals, and Martin [Barre] added the other electric guitar part to it. So it was one of those strange songs—I'm not saying we weren't all in the room at the same time, we were probably all there that day—but it was certainly more like a later Pink Floyd recording than a Jethro Tull recording in that it was made up of a lot of overdubs of parts. And no one knew what the song was going to sound like except me. Sometimes these things that get put together in the studio very artificially end up translating into great live songs and sometimes they really don't.

SONG TITLE The Chain

ARTIST Fleetwood Mac

Featured on Rumours. Released 1977/Reprise
Words & music by Fleetwood Mac

Christine McVie (singer/songwriter):

It was just a melody, and I couldn't find any words to it . . . there's definitely a heavy connection with the "chain." In the end, the chain would keep us together.

Lindsey Buckingham (singer/songwriter/guitarist):

The whole song is like a Brian Wilson. "Good Vibrations" and they just worked.

There's one track on the album that started out as one song in Sausalito. We decided it needed a bridge, so we cut a bridge and edited it into the rest of the song. We didn't get a vocal and left it for a long time in a bunch of pieces. It almost went off the album. Then we listened back and decided we liked the bridge, but didn't like the rest of the song. So I wrote the verse for that bridge, which was originally not in the song and edited those in. We saved the ending. The ending was the only thing left from the original track. We ended up calling it "The Chain" because it was a bunch of pieces.

SONG TITLE Come Together

ARTIST the Beatles

Featured on Abbey Road. Released 1969/Capitol
Words & music by John Lennon and Paul McCartney

John Lennon (singer/songwriter):

The thing was created in the studio. It's gobbledygook; "Come Together" was an expression that Timothy Leary had come up with for his attempt at being president or whatever he wanted to be, and he asked me to write a campaign song. I tried and tried, but I couldn't come up with one. But I came up with this, "Come Together," which would have been no good to him—you couldn't have a campaign song like that, right? . . . It was a funky record—it's one of my favorite Beatle tracks, or, one of my favorite Lennon tracks, let's say that. It's funky, it's bluesy, and I'm singing it pretty well. I like the sound of the record. You can dance to it. I'll buy it!

A Quick One

Songs That Seem to Write Themselves

We all have moments of revelation. There are times when songs have come so quickly to the songwriter that they seem to have written themselves, as if something or someone was pushing the pen to paper.

SONG TITLE Baby, I Love Your Way

ARTIST Peter Frampton

Featured on Frampton Comes Alive! Released 1976/A&M
Words & music by Peter Frampton

Peter Frampton (singer/guitarist/songwriter):

I wrote it in the morning in Nassau. That was when I was writing the Frampton record. I was there for three weeks; two weeks nothing. The last week I wrote the entire record . . . "Show Me the Way" was written in the morning and "Baby, I Love Your Way" was written at sunset the same day. I've often tried to re-create that day! Did I have All-Bran or did I have Raisin Bran? Did I get out of the right side of the bed? What did I do?

SONG TITLE **Satisfaction**

ARTIST **the Rolling Stones**

Featured on Out of Our Heads. Released 1965/ABKCO
Words & music by Mick Jagger and Keith Richards

Mick Jagger (singer/songwriter):

It was Keith really. I mean it was his initial idea. It sounded like a folk song when we first started working on it, and Keith didn't like it very much, he didn't want it to be a single, he didn't think it would do very well . . . I think Keith thought it was a bit basic. I don't think he really listened to it properly. He was too close to it and just felt it was a silly kind of riff.

Keith Richards (songwriter/guitarist):

I wrote that. I woke up one night in a hotel room. Hotel rooms are great. You can do some of your best writing in hotel rooms. I woke up with a riff in my head and the basic refrain, and wrote it down. The record still sounded like a dub to me. I wanted to do . . . I couldn't see getting excited about it. I'd really dug it that night in the hotel, but I'd gone past it. No, I didn't want it out, I said. I wanted to cut it again. It sounded all right, but I didn't really like that fuzz guitar. I wanted to make that thing different. But I don't think we could have done that; you need either horns or something that could really knock that riff out.

SONG TITLE **Excitable Boy**

ARTIST **Warren Zevon**

Featured on Excitable Boy. Released 1978/Asylum
Words & music by Warren Zevon and Leroy Martinelli

Warren Zevon (singer/songwriter):

Roy's [Leroy P. Martinelli] an old friend who's got an amazing sense of humor, and as we were sitting around one day I said, "Roy, how come nobody ever lets me play lead guitar?" And Roy said, "Well, Warren . . . (if you've ever heard me play guitar, you understand the situation) he said, "You get good ideas on the guitar, but . . . then . . . you get . . . excited." To which I replied, "Well, Roy, I'm just an excitable boy," and we laughed and spent the next half hour writing the song.

SONG TITLE **A Hard Day's Night**

ARTIST **the Beatles**

Featured on A Hard Day's Night. Released 1964/Capitol
Words & music by John Lennon and Paul McCartney

Walter Shenson (film producer):

I told John that it would be great to have a song called "A Hard Day's Night" to play over the title and credits . . . he just said he'd think about it. That night we were driving back into town together, and he asked the driver to let him off first because he had some work to do. The next morning at about eight-thirty, John asked me to step aside into this little room. Paul was in there, and they began playing their guitars, singing words John had written out on a matchbook. The song was "A Hard Day's Night."

SONG TITLE **I Saw the Light**

ARTIST Todd Rundgren

Featured on Something/Anything? Released 1972/Bearsville
Words & music by Todd Rundgren

Todd Rundgren (singer/songwriter):

I wrote this song in 15 minutes from start to finish. It was one of the reasons that caused me to change my style of writing. It doesn't matter how clever a song is—if it's written in 15 minutes, it is such a string of clichés that just doesn't have lasting impact for me. And for me, the greatest disappointment in the world is not being able to listen to my own music and enjoy it.

SONG TITLE **Crocodile Rock**

ARTIST Elton John

Featured on Don't Shoot Me I'm Only the Piano Player. Released 1973/MCA
Words & music by Elton John and Bernie Taupin

Elton John (singer/songwriter/pianist):

The music for it was written in less than half an hour . . . I always wanted to write one song, a nostalgic song, a rock and roll song which captured the right sounds. "Crocodile Rock" is just a combination of so many songs, really. "Little Darling," "Oh, Carol," some Beach Boys influences, they're in there as well, I suppose. Eddie Cochran. I mean, it's just a combination of songs.

SONG TITLE **Live and Let Die**

ARTIST **Wings**

Featured on Wings Greatest. Released 1978/Capitol
Words & music by Paul McCartney

Paul McCartney (singer/songwriter/instrumentalist):

When I was asked to do a Bond film, I thought, "Why not?" I said, "Look, give me a week. If I can't do it, I'll back out of it." I don't normally write to titles, for instance. But I read the Bond book the next day, on a Saturday, because they hadn't finished the film, and I wrote the song on a Sunday. I was ready to go with George Martin the next week. I found it came easily.

But when George took it to one of the producers, he said, "That's fine for the demo. When are you gonna record the real thing?" George said, "That's it, boys!" It was one of the best demos we ever made. But it was hard to do, the trick being how to combine my writing with the "Bondiness" of the sound track orchestration riffs. I'll tell you who liked that song, and I was always surprised: Neil Young! He told me, and I said I wouldn't have thought it'd be to his taste.

SONG TITLE **Trampled Underfoot**

ARTIST **Led Zeppelin**

Featured on Physical Graffiti. Released 1975/Swan Song
Words & music by Robert Plant, Jimmy Page and John Paul Jones

Robert Plant (singer/songwriter):

We'd got together to do something entirely different and it just came out. I immediately thought the drive and pace of the thing resembled a car, so I started and wrote two verses while the band was running through it to get it into some order. Then I disappeared upstairs into a bedroom because we were recording at a house, and I wrote the rest of the song in about half an hour. It's a wordplay: "Greasy slick damn body, groovy leather trim/Like the way you hold the road, momma it ain't no sin." Chuck Berry really was the master of that sort of thing.

SONG TITLE **The Low Spark of High Heeled Boys**

ARTIST Traffic

Featured on The Low Spark of High Heeled Boys. Released 1971/Island
Words & music by Steve Winwood and Jim Capaldi

Chris Blackwell (president of Island Records):

The name "Low Spark" is a good example of the way things happen with Traffic. We had the words to the first verse of "Low Spark" on the album cover, but there was no such song. The album was almost complete, and we needed one last cut. Steve Winwood went home to see if he could come up with something. He came back the next day with the song. Jim wrote some more lyrics, and we recorded it in one day. It was very casual, actually.

SONG TITLE **Tuesday Afternoon**

ARTIST the Moody Blues

Featured on Days of Future Passed. Released 1967/Polydor
Words & music by Justin Hayward

Justin Hayward (singer/songwriter/guitarist):

I'd decided I wanted to write a piece about the afternoon. It was a lovely day near where I lived in Swindon, in the west of England. I took my acoustic guitar to the middle of a field and just started writing this song.

SONG TITLE **Welcome to the Machine**

ARTIST Pink Floyd

Featured on Wish You Were Here. Released 1975/Columbia
Words & music by Roger Waters

David Gilmour (singer/songwriter/guitarist):

It's very much a made-up-in-the-studio thing, which was all built up from a basic throbbing made on a VCS3 [synthesizer], with a one repeat echo used so that each "boom" is followed by an echo repeat to give the throb. With a number like that, you don't start off with a regular concept of group structure or anything, and there's no backing track either. Really it is just a studio proposition where we're using tape for its own ends—a form of collage using sound.

Roger Waters (singer/songwriter/bassist):

"Welcome to the Machine" is about "them and us," and anyone who gets involved in the media process.

SONG TITLE **Rock and Roll**

ARTIST Led Zeppelin

Featured on Untitled (Led Zeppelin IV). Released 1971/Swan Song
Words & Music by Robert Plant, Jimmy Page, John Paul Jones and John Bonham

Jimmy Page (guitarist/songwriter):

We were attempting "Four Sticks" and it wasn't happening and Bonzo [John Bonham] started the drum intro to "Keep a Knocking" [by Little Richard] while the tape was still running and I played the riff automatically, that was "Rock and Roll" and we got through the whole first verse. We said this is great, forget "Four Sticks" let's work on this and things were coming out like that. [It] was a spontaneous combustion.

SONG TITLE I'm Your Captain

ARTIST Grand Funk Railroad

Featured on Capitol Collector Series (repackage). Released 1991/Capitol
Words & music by Mark Farner

Mark Farner (singer/songwriter/guitarist):

I said my prayers one night and asked God to give me lyrics to a song that he wanted to touch people's hearts, and lo and behold, in the middle of the night, I wrote "I'm Your Captain." The following morning as I sat in the big kitchen at the farmhouse, I grabbed my axe out of the corner and started strumming. Between sips of coffee, I was moved to play the chord changes that you now recognize in "I'm Your Captain." I went to my bedroom, grabbed the lyrics, brought them back out, and put this song together over a cup of coffee and took it to rehearsal that day. The guys loved it and so do millions of people around the world.

SONG TITLE Rocket Man

ARTIST Elton John

Featured on Honky Chateau. Released 1972/MCA
Words & music by Elton John and Bernie Taupin

Bernie Taupin (lyricist):

The words just came into my head: "She packed my bags last night, preflight. Zero-hour is 9 A.M." I remember jumping out of the car and running into my parents' house, shouting, "Please don't anyone talk to me until I've written this down."

Please Don't Let Me Be Misunderstood

Controversial Lyrics over the Years

Over the years many lyrical messages have been misinterpreted. Sometimes only the songwriters themselves truly understand the deeper, underlying intent behind their words . . .

EAGLES, The: Don Felder and Joe Walsh
(Photo by Anastasia Pantsios)

SONG TITLE Life in the Fast Lane

ARTIST the Eagles

Featured on Hotel California. Released 1976/Asylum
Words & music by Joe Walsh, Glenn Frey and Don Henley

Don Henley (singer/songwriter):

It's mistaken as a song glorifying that type of lifestyle, when in fact it's not. I'm just trying to give others the benefit of my experience! We tried to be careful. We got slammed for all kinds of stuff—for being sexists, the word "misogyny" has come up, which I think is completely ridiculous. People are always looking for something to jab you for. It's very strange to me sometimes the way people interpret songs.

SONG TITLE Don't Fear the Reaper

ARTIST Blue Oyster Cult

Featured on Agents of Fortune. Released 1976/Columbia
Words & music by Buck Dharma

Buck Dharma (singer/songwriter/guitarist):

[The second verse is] the one that's caused all the trouble all these years. Valentine as metaphor for mortal love/stuff, done now. Romeo and Juliet I used as an example of a couple who had faith to take their love elsewhere when (in their case) they weren't permitted the freedom to love here and now. What I meant was, *they're* in eternity, 'cause they had the *faith* to believe in the possibility. It frankly never occurred to me that the suicide aspect of their story would be plugged in (like images in a rock video?) to people's take on "Reaper" making it an advert for suicide. The forty thousand number was pulled from the air as a guess about how many people died every day worldwide, not how many people committed suicide. . . . It never bothered me that "Reaper" was embraced as a horror icon (*Halloween* and *The Stand*) or allegedly enjoyed by Gary Gilmore (*Executioner's Song*). It *would* bother me to know "Reaper" gave someone an excuse to commit suicide. I never have come anywhere close to *really* wanting to commit suicide. I'm gonna live until I die. On the other hand when I go, I don't want "Amazing Grace" as the musical centerpiece at my funeral. I want "Don't Fear the Reaper."

SONG TITLE **My Generation**

ARTIST **the Who**

Featured on The Who Sings My Generation. Released 1966/MCA
Words & music by Peter Townshend

Peter Townshend (songwriter/guitarist):

I remember very clearly when "My Generation" came out, with the words "I hope I die before I get old." I kept being asked, "Do you really mean that? If you are working in five years what will you think?" And I said, "No way am I still going to be doing anything in five years." I really believed that I was going to be dead. There was that huge atomic crisis over Cuba, and I remember in England going to school one day knowing that the world was going to be blown to bits. And in college a lot of people were walking around like normal and occasionally one person would say, "What the fuck are we doing all this for?" Everybody was so resigned to it; they knew there was going to be an atomic war. That was the kind of consciousness at the time. A lot of people have forgotten about it, but I remember the feeling and it lasted for quite a number of years.

SONG TITLE **Get Back**

ARTIST the Beatles

Featured on Let It Be. Released 1970/Capitol
Words & music by John Lennon and Paul McCartney

Paul McCartney (singer/songwriter/instrumentalist):

When we were doing *Let It Be,* there were a couple of verses to "Get Back," which were actually not racist at all—they were antiracist. There were a lot of stories in the newspapers then about Pakistanis crowding out flats—you know, living sixteen to a room or whatever. So in one of the verses of "Get Back," which we were making up on the set of *Let It Be,* one of the outtakes has something about "too many Pakistanis living in a council flat"—that's the line. Which to me was talking out against overcrowding for Pakistanis. . . . If there was any group that was not racist, it was the Beatles. I mean, all our favorite people were always black. We were kind of the first people to open international eyes, in a way, to Motown.

SONG TITLE **Under My Thumb**

ARTIST the Rolling Stones

Featured on Aftermath. Released 1966/ABKCO
Words & music by Mick Jagger and Keith Richards

Mick Jagger (singer/songwriter):

"Under My Thumb," which is always the one they quote, is about a girl who's been real super pushy. People don't think about it 'cause they won't be bothered to listen. It's about "a girl who once had me down." So it's not quite the misogynist view.

It's obvious English people don't take life quite so seriously. They always have a tongue in cheek.

SONG TITLE **Beast of Burden**

ARTIST the Rolling Stones

Featured on Some Girls. Released 1978/Virgin
Words & music by Mick Jagger and Keith Richards

Mick Jagger (singer/songwriter):

I don't want a beast of burden. I don't want the kind of woman who's going to drudge for me. The song says: "I don't need a beast of burden, and I'm not going to be your beast of burden, either." Any woman can see that that's like my saying that I don't want a woman to be on her knees for me. I mean, I get accused of being very anti-girl, right? But people don't really listen, they get it all wrong: they hear "Beast of Burden" and say "Argggh!"

SONG TITLE **Rikki Don't Lose That Number**

ARTIST Steely Dan

Featured on Pretzel Logic. Released 1974/MCA
Words & music by Donald Fagen and Walter Becker

Walter Becker (songwriter):

Some interviewer asked us something about whether the word "number" in the song referred to a marijuana cigarette. I think that's San Francisco slang—or was originally—but we didn't know that.

Donald Fagen (singer/songwriter):

Well, the fact is that we were referring to a phone number, so I think people should take the lyrics more literally and it'll be on the safe side. It's a very simple love song to a young lady. I always thought it was a rather erotic, decadent sort of thing. Here you find a guy—a rather rich gentleman—living in a resort, and somehow he manages to capture this young lady.

SONG TITLE **Dark Star**

ARTIST **Crosby, Stills and Nash**

Featured on CSN. Released 1977/Atlantic
Words & music by Stephen Stills

Stephen Stills (singer/songwriter/guitarist):

Who is "Dark Star" about? This is not *People* magazine. I'd rather maintain the enigma.

SONG TITLE **Go Your Own Way**

ARTIST **Fleetwood Mac**

Featured on Rumours. Released 1977/Reprise
Words & music by Lindsey Buckingham

Stevie Nicks (singer/songwriter):

Now, I want you to know—that line about "shacking up?" I never shacked up with anybody when I was with him [Lindsey Buckingham]! People will hear the song and think that! I was the one who broke up with him. All he wanted to do was fall asleep with that guitar.

SONG TITLE **Behind Blue Eyes**

ARTIST the Who

Featured on Who's Next. Released 1971/MCA
Words & music by Peter Townshend

Peter Townshend (songwriter/guitarist):

"Behind Blue Eyes" is not a song about me. It was written to show how lonely it is for the powerful. Sometimes I write very effectively when I write about things other people feel. I mean, I've got blue eyes and so has Roger Daltrey, but I've never felt that "love was vengeance." It's remarkable how many people just identify with that song from a personal point of view; how everybody feels they're driven to deceit in order to feel love, so that love will always be like vengeance, will always be painful for the recipient. Quite interesting.

SONG TITLE **Hey Jude**

ARTIST the Beatles

Featured on Hey Jude. Released 1970/Capitol
Words & music by John Lennon and Paul McCartney

Paul McCartney (singer/songwriter/instrumentalist):

I happened to be driving out to see Cynthia Lennon. I think it was just after John and she had broken up, and I was quite mates with Julian. He's a nice kid, Julian. And I was going out in me car just vaguely singing this song, and it was like "Hey Jules." I don't know why, "Hey Jules." It was just this thing, you know, "Don't make it bad / Take a sad song . . ." And then I just thought a better name was Jude. A bit more country and western for me.

John Lennon (singer/songwriter/guitarist):

He said it was written about Julian. . . . But I always heard it as a song to me. Now I'm sounding like one of those fans reading things into it. . . . Think about it: Yoko had just come into the picture. He is saying, "Hey John." Subconsciously, he was saying, go ahead, leave me. On a conscious level, he didn't want me to go ahead.

SONG TITLE **Killer Queen**

ARTIST Queen

Featured on Sheer Heart Attack. Released 1974/Hollywood (rerelease)
Words & music by Freddie Mercury

Freddie Mercury (singer/songwriter):

A lot of people thought "Killer Queen" was about Jackie Kennedy. It wasn't. The critics invented that.

It's about a high-class call girl. I'm trying to say that classy people can be whores as well. That's what the song is about, though I'd prefer people to put their own interpretation upon it—to read what they like into it.

SONG TITLE **La Grange**

ARTIST ZZ Top

Featured on Tres Hombres. Released 1973/Warner Brothers
Words & music by Billy Gibbons, Frank Gibbons and Dusty Hill

Billy Gibbons (songwriter/guitarist):

La Grange, Texas, was the notorious locale for one of the most illustrious cathouses in the state. You just mention La Grange, and most people would certainly be able to raise an eyebrow over it. That tune was written probably farther back than I care to elaborate on. We put it together and shortly after the release, notoriety came to La Grange after an overzealous newsman took it upon himself to expose what was going on, and in one short week, a many, many year old tradition was on the rocks. There were many tears shed over the demise of that particular establishment. I think we're still waving a little bit of the Texas flag when we play that particular cut. It's certainly our statement about having a good time at the place.

SONG TITLE Lola

ARTIST the Kinks

Featured on Lola Versus Powerman and the Moneygoround, Part One.
Released 1970/Reprise
Words & music by Ray Davies

Ray Davies (singer/songwriter/guitarist):
"Lola" is a long, long story. A subject for a glossy paperback. It's the kind of torment that anybody in that situation goes through. I was desperate to make my marriage work. It's all too easy to say that you're imprisoned by the people who love you. But I was making myself a prisoner, and I wasn't able to do my job properly, that's all there is. I remember Rasa got very upset when she said that "Lola" was the first single she hadn't sung on. I remember an incident in a club. I think Robert Wace had been dancing with this black woman, and he said, "I'm really on to a thing here." And it was OK until we left at six in the morning, and then I said, "Have you seen the stubble?" He said, "Yeah," but he was too pissed to care, I think. I'd had a few dances with it . . . him. It's kind of obvious. It's that thrust in the pelvic region when they're on the dance floor, and they're never quite the same as a woman. So it's a combined disguise. But "Lola" is a love song.

At the turn of the year, I felt very dejected, very depressed. I was offered a part in a play and I took it. It was called *The Long-Distance Piano Player*, and it cleared me of all music. I came back refreshed and energized. I had two songs, "Lola" and "Powerman." We rehearsed in the front room of Fortis Green for weeks and weeks. Then we went and recorded it. We did one version, and Bob Wace said, "What you need is a really arrested beginning, like you used to have on 'You Really Got Me.' " So I got the first few chords, strummed the guitar, then started the lyric.

SONG TITLE Being For the Benefit of Mr. Kite

ARTIST the Beatles

Featured on Sgt. Pepper's Lonely Hearts Club Band. Released 1967/Capitol
Words & music by John Lennon and Paul McCartney

John Lennon (singer/songwriter):

The whole song is from a Victorian poster, which I bought in a junk shop. It is so cosmically beautiful. It's a poster for a fair that must have happened in the 1800s. Everything in the song is from that poster, except the horse wasn't called Henry. Now, there were all kinds of stories about Henry the Horse being heroin. I had never seen heroin in that period. No, it's all just from that poster. The song is pure, like painting, a pure watercolor.

SONG TITLE The Pusher

ARTIST Steppenwolf

Featured on Steppenwolf. Released 1973/MCA
Words & music by H. Axton

John Kay (singer/songwriter):

We were occasionally picketed in the South outside the venue by church groups protesting our song "The Pusher," insisting we were taking the Lord's name in vain. Once, in Winston-Salem, North Carolina, we were scheduled to play the War Memorial Arena, 9,000 people, sold out. At the airport we were met by the mayor, police chief, and the fire chief, who were very pleasant and congenial but who had come to inform us of the following problem: a fundamentalist Baptist preacher [had come to them demanding] we must delete certain songs, one of them being "The Pusher." We were getting the vibe from these people that they thought this preacher was an asshole but they had to throw him a bone. Finally, they concluded that we couldn't sing the line "God damn the pusher."

Just prior to this incident, we had received an excerpt from an article written by a clergyman for one of the Baptist publications explaining that "The Pusher" was not only anti-drug but that the phrase "god damn" was being used in the true biblical context—may God damn the pusher for what he does. He was the first one to have the insight to see the obvious. . . . We went on that night, the crowd was really into it, boisterous and loud, and we went down well. When it was encore time, we went back up and I addressed the crowd: "Unbeknownst to you, there was a good chance that we would not play tonight. You guys would have all had to get your money back, and it would have been a real drag for everyone. There were certain demands put on us by the municipal power structure here in terms of what we could and could not play. . . . Now, I have more or less promised that I will not sing two very important words out of "The Pusher." But you guys didn't promise anything like that. It's up to you." We started into the song, and every time I was supposed to do "god damn" there arose 9,000 voices shouting at the top of their lungs, "GOD DAMN THE PUSHER." You've never seen so many red faces backstage. They didn't have to arrest me, I didn't cop to their power game, and the crowd got a buzz out of it.

SONG TITLE Sweet Home Alabama

ARTIST Lynyrd Skynyrd

Featured on Second Helping. Released 1974/MCA
Words & music by Ronnie Van Zant, Edward King and Gary Rossington

Gary Rossington (songwriter/guitarist):

We listened to Neil Young a lot back then, and "Southern Man" really cut the South—and he's from Canada! It kind of peeved us, so we wrote that—kind of as a joke. We never thought it would be a single, much less a hit . . . nothing we did was that premeditated.

SONG TITLE No More Mr. Nice Guy

ARTIST Alice Cooper

Featured on Billion Dollar Babies. Released 1973/Warner Brothers
Words & music by Alice Cooper and M. Bruce

Alice Cooper (singer/songwriter):

That has a Who open chord feel to it. It was a real basic song with a funny lyric. Every time we came into a different town, there were new rumors about us. We figured everyone hated us so much, we would take it to the extreme—"you think we are bad now, wait until you see what's coming!"

SONG TITLE Free Man in Paris

ARTIST Joni Mitchell

Featured on Court & Spark. Released 1974/Asylum
Words & music by Joni Mitchell

Joni Mitchell (singer/songwriter):

People assume that everything I write is autobiographical. If I sing in the first person, they think it's all about me. With a song like "Free Man in Paris" they attribute almost every word of the song to my personal life, somehow missing the setups of "He said" and "She said." Certainly, most of the song is eyewitness accounting, but many of the characters I write about—even if their tone is entirely first-person—have nothing to do with my own life in the intimate sense. It's more like dramatic recitation or theatrical soliloquy.

Really Deep Thoughts

Songwriters Contemplate Life, Music, War, Etc.

Occasionally rock artists have been known to muse about the bigger picture in life. They contemplate a range of serious topics such as mortality, religion, stardom and other intensely personal experiences through their songwriting.

SONG TITLE Daniel

ARTIST Elton John

Featured on Don't Shoot Me I'm Only the Piano Player. Released 1973/MCA
Words & music by Elton John and Bernie Taupin

Bernie Taupin (lyricist):

I forget now if it was *Time* or *Newsweek*—it was about this guy who'd been wounded in the Vietnam War and had gone back to his hometown, just wanting to forget it all and get on with his life. But the people then wanted him to be a hero and wouldn't leave him alone. In the end, this guy had become so disillusioned, he'd decided the only way out was to leave America altogether . . . I wrote this thing "Daniel," in about half an hour and took it to Elton. Elton got up from the breakfast table, went over to the piano, and finished it in about 15 to 20 minutes, then said to the band, "Hey, guys, let's cut this." We'd done the track by the end of the day.

SONG TITLE **American Pie**

ARTIST Don McLean

Featured on American Pie. Released 1971/EMI
Words & music by Don McLean

Don McLean (singer/songwriter):

I was quite interested in America—I still write about the different aspects of America—and to me, something was slipping away, and I couldn't quite put my finger on how to express it. I was sitting up in this little house where I lived, and I just started to write this first verse about the day I cut open this bunch of papers [he was a paperboy] and saw that Buddy Holly'd been killed. The memory unlocked a whole bunch of things. Suddenly the song wrote itself.

I was in love with Buddy and his music. And I remember sadly that by 1964, you didn't hear anything about Buddy Holly. He was completely forgotten. But I didn't forget him. And whenever I'd find one of his songs on a jukebox, or find an odd record that I didn't have, I'd grab it . . . I think this song helped make people aware that Buddy's legitimate musical contribution had been overlooked. Of course, the Beatles didn't overlook it, and other people hadn't overlooked it, but the public at large wasn't aware of where he fit on the old rock and roll tree. . . . When I first heard "American Pie" on the radio, I was playing a gig somewhere, and it was immediately followed by "Peggy Sue." They caught on to the Holly connection right away, and that made me very happy.

SONG TITLE **Edge of Seventeen**

ARTIST **Stevie Nicks**

Featured on Bella Donna. Released 1981/Modern
Words & music by Stevie Nicks

Stevie Nicks (singer/songwriter):

The line "And the days go by like a strand in the wind"—that's how fast those days were going by during my uncle's illness, and it was so upsetting to me. The part that says "I went today . . . maybe I will go again . . . tomorrow" refers to seeing him the day before he died. He was home, and my aunt had some music softly playing, and it was a perfect place for the spirit to go away. The "white-winged dove" in the song is a spirit that is leaving a body, and I felt a great loss at how both Johns [her uncle and John Lennon] were taken. "I hear the call of the night bird singing come away . . . come away. . . ."

SONG TITLE **The End**

ARTIST the Doors

Featured on The Doors. Released 1967/Elektra
Words & music by the Doors

Jim Morrison (singer/songwriter):

I went to a movie one night in Westwood, and I was in a bookstore or some shop where they sell pottery and calendars and gadgets, y'know . . . and a very attractive, intelligent—intelligent in the sense of aware and open—girl thought she recognized me, and she came to say hello. And she was asking me about that particular song. She was just out for a little stroll with a nurse. She was on leave, just for an hour or so, from the UCLA Neuropsychiatric Institute. She lived there and was just out for a walk. Apparently, she had been a student at UCLA and freaked on heavy drugs or something. Anyway, she said that that song was really a favorite of a lot of kids in her ward. At first I thought, "Oh, man . . . "—and this was after I talked with her for a while, saying it could mean a lot of things, kind of a maze or a puzzle to think about, everybody should relate it to their own situation. I didn't realize people took songs so seriously, and it made me wonder whether I ought to consider the consequences.

SONG TITLE **That Smell**

ARTIST Lynyrd Skynyrd

Featured on Street Survivors. Released 1977/MCA
Words & music by Ronnie Van Zant and Allen Collins

Ronnie Van Zant (singer/songwriter):

I wrote that song when Gary had his car accident. It was last year, and Allan and Billy also were in car accidents, all in the space of six months, so I had a creepy feeling things were going against us, so I thought I'd write a morbid song.

SONG TITLE **Someone Saved My Life Tonight**

ARTIST **Elton John**

Featured on Captain Fantastic and the Brown Dirt Cowboy. Released 1975/MCA
Words & music by Elton John and Bernie Taupin

Bernie Taupin (lyricist):

Elton was destined to tie the knot. And I don't think he was very sure about it. He was getting more and more depressed. He talked about going to end it all. I was totally sympathetic too and said, "Yeah, right!" I was coming out of my room and walking down the hall when I smelled gas—someone had left the oven on in the kitchen. I walk into the kitchen and there's Elton lying on the floor with the gas oven open. And my immediate thing should have been, "My, God, he's tried to kill himself." The thing was I started laughing, because he'd taken a pillow . . . and he'd opened all the windows!

SONG TITLE **Uncle Albert/Admiral Halsey**

ARTIST Paul McCartney

Featured on Ram. Released 1971/Capitol
Words & music by Paul McCartney

Paul McCartney (singer/songwriter/instrumentalist):

I had an Uncle Albert; I was sort of thinking of him. He was an uncle who died when I was a kid, a good bloke who used to get drunk and stand on the table and read passages from the Bible, at which point people used to laugh. *A lot.* It was just one of those things—"Ohh, Albert, don't get up and read the Bible again! Shut up! Sit down!!" But he's someone I recalled fondly, and when the song was coming, it was like a nostalgic thing. "I think I'm gonna rain" was the wistful line, really, and I thought of him.

I say, I never can explain why I think of a particular person when I write. "We're so sorry, Auntie Edna"—you know, it could have been her. As for Admiral Halsey, he's one of yours, an American admiral. I could have gone, "Gen-e-ral Ei-sen-how-er," but it doesn't work as well. And then people say, "Ah-hah! I know why he used Halsey. In the Battle of Salaami in Nineteen-Forty-Hee-Hee he was instrumental in—" None of that sort of bit is hardly ever true. I use these things like a painter uses colors. I don't know where I got Halsey's name, but you read it in magazines and sometimes they just fall into your songs because they scan so well.

SONG TITLE **Funeral For a Friend**

ARTIST Elton John

Featured on Goodbye Yellow Brick Road. Released 1973/MCA
Music by Elton John

Elton John (singer/songwriter/pianist):

Gus Dudgeon (producer) had always said I should do an instrumental. One day I was feeling really down, and I said to myself, "What kind of music would I like to hear at my own funeral?" I'd always liked funeral music anyway. I like very sad music of any kind.

SONG TITLE **Southern Cross**

ARTIST Crosby, Still and Nash

Featured on Daylight Again. Released 1982/Atlantic
Words & music by Stephen Stills, Richard Curtis and Michael Curtis

Stephen Stills (singer/songwriter/guitarist):

The Curtis Brothers brought a wonderful song called "Seven League Boots," but it drifted around too much. I rewrote a new set of words and added a different chorus, a story about a long boat trip I took after my divorce. It's about using the power of the universe to heal your wounds. Once again, I was given somebody's gem and cut and polished it.

SONG TITLE **Hey Joe**

ARTIST Jimi Hendrix

Featured on Are You Experienced? Released 1967/Reprise
Traditional; arrangement by the Jimi Hendrix Experience

Jimi Hendrix (singer/songwriter/guitarist):

"Hey Joe" is a blues arrangement of a cowboy song that's about a hundred years old. It wasn't being played too much, but I really like it. It's about a cat, he shoots his old lady because he catched her doin' wrong, she's messin' with everybody else. Then after he shoots her, he has to run out of town, go to Mexico where he can be free.

SONG TITLE Help!

ARTIST the Beatles

Featured on Help! Released 1965/Capitol
Words & music by John Lennon and Paul McCartney

John Lennon (singer/songwriter/guitarist):

When "Help!" came out in '65, I was actually crying out for help. Most people think it's just a fast rock 'n' roll song. I didn't realize it at the time; I just wrote the song because I was commissioned to write it for the movie. But later, I knew I really was crying out for help. It was my fat Elvis period. You see the movie: He—I—is very fat, very insecure, and he's completely lost himself. And I am singing about when I was so much younger and all the rest, looking back at how easy it was . . . I was fat and depressed and I was crying out for help.

SONG TITLE Hey You

ARTIST Pink Floyd

Featured on The Wall. Released 1979/Columbia
Words & music by Roger Waters

Roger Waters (singer/songwriter):

"Hey You" is a cry to the rest of the world, you know saying, hey, this isn't right. . . . Dave sings the first two verses of it and then there's an instrumental passage and then there's a bit that goes "but it was only fantasy," which I sing . . . a narration of the thing. "The wall was too high as you can see, no matter how he tried he could not break free and the worms ate into his brain." The worms. That's the first reference to worms . . . the worms have a lot less to do with the piece then they did a year ago; a year ago they were very much a part of it, if you like they were my symbolic representation of decay. Because the basic idea of the whole thing really is that if you isolate yourself you decay.

SONG TITLE **Bodhisattva**

ARTIST **Steely Dan**

Featured on Countdown to Ecstasy. Released 1973/MCA
Words & music by Donald Fagen and Walter Becker

Donald Fagen (singer/songwriter):

That's sort of a parody on the way Western people look at Eastern religion—sort of oversimplify it. We thought it was rather amusing—most people don't get it.

SONG TITLE **Long Distance Runaround**

ARTIST **Yes**

Featured on Fragile. Released 1972/Atlantic
Words & music by Jon Anderson

Jon Anderson (singer/songwriter):

It was how religion had seemed to confuse me totally. It was such a game that seemed to be played, and I was going around in circles looking for the sound of reality, the sound of God. That was my interpretation of that song, that I was always confused. I could never understand the things that religion stood for. And that throughout the years has always popped its head up in the songs I've been working with.

SONG TITLE **The Weight**

ARTIST **the Band**

Featured on Music from Big Pink. Released 1968/Capitol
Words & music by Robbie Robertson

Robbie Robertson (singer/songwriter):

It was recorded only as an afterthought for *Big Pink*. "The Weight" was, like, "Okay, this doesn't have a very complicated chord progression, it's just kind of traditional, so we'll cut that when we get stuck for a song." And then when we cut it and thought, "Gee, it's kind of effective when you hear it back at you like that . . ." It's about the impossibility of sainthood.

SONG TITLE **Woodstock**

ARTIST Crosby, Stills, Nash and Young

Featured on Déjà Vu. Released 1970/Atlantic
Words & music by Joni Mitchell

Joni Mitchell (singer/songwriter):

The deprivation of not being able to go provided me with an intense angle on Woodstock. I was one of the fans. I was put in the position of being a kid who couldn't make it. So I was glued to the media. And at the time I was going through a kind of born-again Christian trip—not that I went to any church. I'd given up Christianity at a very early age in Sunday school. But suddenly, as performers, we were in the position of having so many people look to us for leadership, and for some unknown reason, I took it seriously and decided I needed a guide and leaned on God. So I was a little "God mad" at the time, for lack of a better term, and I had been saying to myself, "Where are the modern miracles?" Woodstock, for some reason, impressed me as being a modern miracle, like a modern-day fishes-and-loaves story. For a herd of people that large to cooperate so well, it was pretty remarkable and there was tremendous optimism. So I wrote the song "Woodstock" out of these feelings, and the first three times I performed it in public, I burst into tears, because it brought back the intensity of the experience and was so moving.

Graham Nash (singer/songwriter):

It was such a great song, the whole feeling of the song . . . it pinned exactly what had happened, in terms of being in a wheel in something turning. As soon as the four of us heard it, we wanted to do that record so bad. And we did.

SONG TITLE Limelight

ARTIST Rush

Featured on Moving Pictures. Released 1981/Mercury
Words & music by Geddy Lee, Alex Lifeson and Neil Peart

Alex Lifeson (guitarist/songwriter):

"Limelight" is about being under the microscopic scrutiny of the public and the need for privacy—trying to separate the two and not always being successful at it. Because we've never been a high-profile band, we've managed to retain a lot of our privacy. But we've had to work at it. Neil's [Peart, drummer and lyricist] very militant about his privacy.

SONG TITLE Minstrel in the Gallery

ARTIST Jethro Tull

Featured on Minstrel in the Gallery. Released 1975/Chrysalis
Words & music by Ian Anderson and Martin Barre

Ian Anderson (singer/songwriter/instrumentalist):

It's all about how I'm up there on stage and they're all down there [in the gallery] and how it really amazes me that I don't alienate everybody by what I sing about. Either they don't understand or they give me the benefit of a lot of doubt. . . . In the sense that to earn a living, we play anywhere and everywhere there are people, we are akin to the minstrels of old.

SONG TITLE Eight Miles High

ARTIST the Byrds

Featured on Fifth Dimension. Released 1966/Columbia
Words & music by Gene Clark, David Crosby and Roger McGuinn

Roger McGuinn (singer/songwriter/guitarist):

We were on a tour over in England, and we had a rough time with the press over there. . . . They slaughtered us, said we were terrible. In fact, we weren't that great as a live band; we were a little loose onstage. But we weren't as bad as they said; they gave us a real hard time. So when we got back, we thought we'd write a musical impression of our trip. Basically, it's about the altitude of the airplane—eight miles high—and when you land over there, "when you touch down," you find cultural shock. If you listen to the words, it's all about "The gray town known for its sound, in places small faces unbound," which is all the little girls screaming, and all that.

There's no overdubs on that; it's one straightforward guitar part on a twelve-string. The reason it sounds like that is because I was influenced by John Coltrane. We were on a bus tour before we went to England, and we only had one tape with us. It had John Coltrane on one side and Ravi Shankar on the other. If you listen to Coltrane's India and Africa album, you'll hear a tremendous similarity to the guitar part on "Eight Miles High."

SONG TITLE **Pinball Wizard**

ARTIST **the Who**

Featured on Tommy. Released 1969/MCA
Words & music by Peter Townshend

Peter Townshend (singer/songwriter/guitarist):

It's about life's games, playing the machine—the boy and his machine, the disciples with theirs, the scores, results, colors, vibrations, and actions. I don't happen to be divine at the moment. I can't express the magnificence of divinity in music, but I can express the grooviness of being a pinball champ, because I'm a pop star, which is very close. The absurdity of being a pinball champion!

Elton John (singer/songwriter/pianist):

They tried to cast *Tommy* for a long time, and Rod Stewart rang me up one day, said, "They wanted me to be the Pinball Wizard." I said, "Don't touch it with a barge pole." So about a year later, Pete Townshend rang me up and said, "Will you sing 'Pinball Wizard'?" And I said, "All right—it's a great song and I can't really go wrong," and of course I did it and it was an amazing success, the film and the "Pinball Wizard" track and I don't think Rod's quite forgiven me for that.

SONG TITLE **So You Want to Be a Rock and Roll Star**

ARTIST the Byrds

Featured on Younger than Yesterday. Released 1967/Columbia
Words & music by Roger McGuinn and Chris Hillman

Roger McGuinn (singer/songwriter/guitarist):

The inspiration for that song came from a guitar riff that Millard Thomas, one of the guitar players from the Belafonte singers who played behind Miriam Makeba, used to play. And I showed it to [Chris] Hillman one day and he liked it.

We happened to be looking through this teen magazine at the time and cracking up on how people turned over in this business. Like next week there'd be another batch of, you know, rock and roll people. And we thought, "Let's write a satirical song on that."

SONG TITLE **The Grand Illusion**

ARTIST Styx

Featured on The Grand Illusion. Released 1977/A&M
Words & music by Dennis DeYoung

Tommy Shaw (singer/songwriter/guitarist):

It was such a pertinent and personal thing with all of us at the time. This profession can really play tricks on your head by the fact that you're out there on the stage being what everybody wants you to be but behind that facade you're still trying to be the same person you've always been.

SONG TITLE **The Immigrant Song**

ARTIST **Led Zeppelin**

Featured on Led Zeppelin III. Released 1970/Atlantic
Words & music by Robert Plant and Jimmy Page

Robert Plant (singer/songwriter):

"The hammer of the gods will drive our ships to new lands to fight the horde and see men cry / Valhalla I am coming . . ." That's Led Zeppelin. Yeah, it's gotta be a real adventure, whether it be wandering around the back streets of Bangkok at 2:00 A.M. looking for a whorehouse or staring across the new frontier . . . I mean it's OK being the swashbuckling rock 'n roller, but who got the best, who dug it the most, Elvis Presley or Marco Polo?

History is a big pull on me so in "Immigrant Song" I was wondering about the ancient characters from whence we stemmed, and what they were like, and what they thought about, and how they sung their song . . . whether they sat down and thought: "Well, we've got to top the last one."

SONG TITLE Desperado

ARTIST the Eagles

Featured on Desperado. Released 1973/Asylum
Words & music by Don Henley and Glenn Frey

Don Henley (singer/songwriter):

The whole metaphor of "rock musicians-as-outlaw" seems silly. It wasn't really accurate. I mean we did live outside the laws of normality, but we didn't kill people. At the time, it was fine because that kind of music was getting popular and the image helped get the music across, I think. It holds up musically.

It's funny—growing up in Texas I never paid any attention to all the stories about outlaws. Actually, where the whole concept of that album came from was this book that Jackson Browne, J. D. Souther, Ned Doheny, and Glenn had. It was fun at the time, but unfortunately we got typecast from that album and we were never really able to break out of it, even with *One of These Nights* and *Hotel California* and all our attempts at white R & B and soul music. We were always typecast as a country-rock band on the strength of our first three albums.

SONG TITLE Wasted on the Way

ARTIST Crosby, Stills and Nash

Featured on Daylight Again. Released 1982/Atlantic
Words & music by Graham Nash

Graham Nash (singer/songwriter):

My point on "Wasted on the Way" is just that. We have wasted an enormous amount of time on petty issues that should never have kept us from making music.

SONG TITLE Don't Stop

ARTIST Fleetwood Mac

Featured on Rumours. Released 1977/Reprise
Words & music by Christine McVie

Christine McVie (singer/songwriter/pianist):

"Don't Stop" was just a feeling. It just seemed to be a pleasant revelation to have that "yesterday's gone" and it might have, I guess, been directed more toward John, but I'm just definitely not a pessimist.

SONG TITLE Here Comes the Sun

ARTIST the Beatles

Featured on Abbey Road. Released 1969/Capitol
Words & music by George Harrison

George Harrison (singer/songwriter/guitarist):

This was written at the time [1969] when Apple was getting like school, where we had to go and be businessmen, all this signing accounts, and "sign this" and "sign that." Anyway, it seems as if winter in England goes on forever; by the time spring comes you really deserve it. So one day I decided—I'm going to "sag off" Apple—and I went over to Eric [Clapton]'s house. I was walking in his garden. The relief of not having to go and see all those dopey accountants was wonderful, and I was walking around the garden with one of Eric's acoustic guitars and wrote, "Here Comes the Sun."

SONG TITLE **Running on Empty**

ARTIST **Jackson Browne**

Featured on Running on Empty. Released 1977/Asylum
Words & music by Jackson Browne

Jackson Browne (singer/songwriter):

This is going to sound silly, but I was always driving around with no gas in the car and that's when I started writing the song. I was sort of humming it, you know. When I was making *The Pretender*, I put my own personal oil stains on certain streets in Los Angeles. Night after night, I only drove from my house to the studio and back, and it became so familiar it was like walking down a corridor. I never bothered to fill up the tank because—how far was it anyway? Just a few blocks.

SONG TITLE **The Battle of Evermore**

ARTIST **Led Zeppelin**

Featured on Untitled (Led Zeppelin IV). Released 1971/Swan Song
Words & music by Robert Plant and Jimmy Page

Robert Plant (singer/songwriter):

I had been reading a book on the Scottish wars immediately before. It was really more of a playlet rather than a song, and after I wrote the lyrics, I realized I needed a completely different voice as well as my own. So I asked Sandy Denny along to sing on that track. I found it very satisfying to sing with someone who has a completely different style to my own. While I sang about the events of the song, Sandy answered back as if she was the pulse of the people in the battlements. Sandy was the town crier, urging the people to lay down their weapons.

Jimmy Page (songwriter/guitarist):

I forget whether people had gone to bed early or what, but it just came out then. I picked up the mandolin, which was actually John Paul Jones's mandolin and those chords just came out. It was my first experiment with the mandolin. I suppose all mandolin players would have a great laugh 'cos it must be the standard thing to play those chords, you know, but possibly not the same approach. Anyway it was just one of those things where I was governed by the limitations of the instrument. Possibly, afterwards, it sounded like a dance around the maypole number I must admit, but it wasn't purposely like that—"Let's do a folky number."

That's fingerpicking again, going on back to studio days and developing a certain amount of technique. At least enough to be adapted and used. My fingerpicking is a sort of cross between Pete Seeger, Earl Scruggs, and total incompetence.

SONG TITLE **Wooden Ships**

ARTIST Crosby, Stills and Nash

Featured on Crosby, Stills and Nash. Released 1969/Atlantic
Words & music by David Crosby, Stephen Stills and Paul Kanter

David Crosby (singer/songwriter):

Written in the main cabin of my boat in Mayan. I had the music. Paul Kanter wrote two verses, Stephen wrote one, and I added the bits at both ends. I borrowed the first part off a little Baptist church sign in Florida that said, "If you smile at me I will understand, because that is something everybody everywhere does in the same language." It's a weird science fiction story, but one that could happen tomorrow. "Silver people on the shoreline" are guys in radiation suits. We imagined ourselves as the few survivors, escaping on a boat to create a new civilization. Later on, Jackson Browne said, "What about all the people who get left behind?" and wrote "For Everyone" in response.

SONG TITLE **Ziggy Stardust**

ARTIST David Bowie

Featured on The Rise & Fall of Ziggy Stardust. Released 1972/Rykodisc (rerelease)
Words & music by David Bowie

David Bowie (singer/songwriter):

"Ziggy" was my Martian messiah who twanged a guitar. He was a simplistic character. I saw him as very simple . . . fairly like the character Newton I was to do in the film [*The Man Who Fell to Earth*] later on. Someone who dropped down here, got brought down to our way of thinking, and ended up destroying his own self. Which is a pretty archetype story line.

SONG TITLE **Pretzel Logic**

ARTIST Steely Dan

Featured on Pretzel Logic. Released 1974/MCA
Words & music by Donald Fagen and Walter Becker

Donald Fagen (singer/songwriter):

When it says, "I stepped up on the platform / the man gave me the news," we conceived the platform as a teleportation platform. And there are other key lines like: "I have never met Napoleon, but I plan to find the time." What we're actually saying is I plan to find the time in which he lived.

SONG TITLE **Rhiannon**

ARTIST Fleetwood Mac

Featured on Fleetwood Mac. Released 1975/Reprise
Words & music by Stevie Nicks

Stevie Nicks (singer/songwriter):

I see her as a good witch. Very positive. I sink into that whole trip when I'm onstage.

The legend of Rhiannon is about the song of the birds that take away pain and relieve suffering. That's what music is to me. I don't want any pain. . . . She is some sort of reality. If I didn't know she was a mythological character, I would think maybe she lived down the street.

SONG TITLE Kashmir

ARTIST Led Zeppelin

Featured on Physical Graffiti. Released 1975/Swan Song
Words & music by Jimmy Page, Robert Plant, and John Bonham

Robert Plant (singer/songwriter):

I went to Morocco. It was the first time I started getting away to other lands without an entourage of people or as a member of a band. It was just over a year ago, and the nearer I got to the Sahara, this atmosphere beckoned me to open my eyes in another way. I wrote the first verse before we had any music, I just started to write a poem: "Let the sun beat down upon my face, and stars to fill my dreams / I am a traveler of both time and space, to be where I have been." The people in the mountains, the Berbers and the people beyond there, have all these dances to Pan, and I knew they were there. Occasionally you could ride into the hills and see these people watching as you went by, and you got this fantastic feeling, as if you were going through a no-man's land between Kashmir and India . . . at the end of the song I'm almost satisfied as if I've just done the whole trip. To me, it's just like painting pictures, like "Stairway to Heaven."

SONG TITLE **Proud Mary**

ARTIST Creedence Clearwater Revival

Featured on Bayou Country. Released 1969/Fantasy
Words & music by John Fogerty

John Fogerty (singer/songwriter/guitarist):

One day I was coming into my apartment, and I look on the stairs and, "Hey, that's got my name on it!" Well, son of a bitch, I opened it up and I'm discharged from the army. Holy hallelujah! I actually went out on the little apartment-building lawn and did a couple of cartwheels. At that one moment it was like, "Wow, all the troubles of the world have been lifted off my shoulders!"

If it didn't happen within five minutes, certainly within a week and a half I had written "Proud Mary." That one event that led to doing the cartwheels, that's where "Left a good job in the city" comes from. I just felt real good.

Although I didn't recall it at the time when I was doing "Rollin' on the river," there is an old Will Rogers movie about these old paddle wheelers, and I believe at one point they actually sing, "Rolling on the river." I know that buried deep inside me are all these little bits and pieces of Americana. It's deep in my heart, deep in my soul. As I learned in English 101, write about what you know about.

SONG TITLE **Rock and Roll Never Forgets**

ARTIST Bob Seger

Featured on Night Moves. Released 1976/Capitol
Words & music by Bob Seger

Bob Seger (singer/songwriter):

I got the idea from a reunion that I didn't go to, but a close friend of mine did. And he said I wouldn't have believed those people. They all weighed 500 pounds, and they were as straight as hell. The same guys I used to hang out with! And I started thinking, whenever we go to a concert we see mostly young people . . . I wanted to bring back people my own age, write a song for them.

SONG TITLE **We Are the Champions**

ARTIST Queen

Featured on News of the World. Released 1977/Hollywood (rerelease)
Words & music by Freddie Mercury

Freddie Mercury (singer/songwriter):

I was thinking about football when I wrote it. I wanted a participation song, something the fans could latch onto. It was aimed at the masses; I thought we'd see how they took it. It worked a treat. When we performed it at a private concert in London, the fans actually broke into a football chant between numbers. Of course, I've given it more theatrical subtlety than an ordinary football chant.

Brian May (songwriter/guitarist):

This song is very theatrical. Freddie is very close to his art. You could say, he's married to his music, whether it's "I Did It My Way" or his "There's No Business Like Show Business." I must say, when he first played it for us in the studio we all fell on the floor with laughter. So many of the people in the press hate us because we've sidestepped them and got where we have without them.

But there's no way the song says anything against our audiences. When the song says "we," it means "us and the fans." When we did that special concert [where the song was first performed], the fans were wonderful. They understood it so well. I know it sounds corny, but it brought tears to our eyes.

SONG TITLE Amazing Journey

ARTIST the Who

Featured on Tommy. Released 1969/MCA
Words & music by Peter Townshend

Peter Townshend (singer/songwriter/guitarist):

The pivotal song [to *Tommy*] was "Amazing Journey." That was the song . . . that tries to tell the whole story. It tries to be the introduction to *Tommy.* As soon as I'd written that, I then had the shape for the piece.

SONG TITLE Imagine

ARTIST John Lennon

Featured on Imagine. Released 1971/Capitol
Words & music by John Lennon

John Lennon (singer/songwriter):

"Imagine" is a big hit almost everywhere—antireligious, antinationalistic, anticonventional, anticapitalistic but because it is sugar-coated, it is accepted. Now I understand what you have to do. Put your political message across with a little honey.

JETHRO TULL: members Ian Anderson
and Martin Barre (Photo by Josef M. Astro)

SONG TITLE Thick as a Brick

ARTIST Jethro Tull

Featured on Thick as a Brick. Released 1972/Chrysalis
Words & music by Ian Anderson

Ian Anderson (singer/songwriter/instrumentalist):

That was something that derived from things I was fiddling around with while I was on tour in the U.S. . . . "Thick" was a deliberate attempt to come up with what Saddam Hussein might have referred to as "the mother of all concept albums." It was all delivered tongue in cheek, particularly in terms of its live performance. We delivered it in a way in which people were clearly not sure whether it was a very serious exercise or whether it was a bit of light comedy. In truth, it was both of those things.

SONG TITLE **Saturday Night's Alright For Fighting**

ARTIST Elton John

Featured on Goodbye Yellow Brick Road. Released 1973/MCA
Words & music by Elton John and Bernie Taupin

Bernie Taupin (lyricist):

I'd started to feel I was writing too much about American culture and American things. "Saturday Night's Alright . . ." was my first attempt to write a rock and roll song that was totally English.

SONG TITLE **Strawberry Fields Forever**

ARTIST the Beatles

Featured on Magical Mystery Tour. Released 1967/Capitol
Words & music by John Lennon and Paul McCartney

John Lennon (singer/songwriter/guitarist):

The awareness apparently trying to be expressed is—let's say in one way I was always hip. I was hip in kindergarten. I was different from the others. I was different all my life. The second verse goes, "No one I think is in my tree." Well, I was too shy and self-doubting. Nobody seems to be as hip as me is what I was saying. Therefore, I must be crazy or a genius—"I mean it must be high or low," the next line. There was something wrong with me, I thought, because I seemed to see things other people didn't see. I thought I was crazy or an egomaniac for claiming to see things other people didn't see.

SONG TITLE **The Song Remains the Same**

ARTIST Led Zeppelin

Featured on Houses of the Holy. Released 1973/Atlantic
Words & music by Jimmy Page and Robert Plant

Robert Plant (singer/songwriter):

Every time I sing that, I just picture the fact I've been round and round the world, and at the root of it all there's a common denominator for everybody. The common denominator is what makes it good or bad. Whether it's a Led Zeppelin or an Alice Cooper. The lyrics I'm proud of. Somebody pushed my pen for me, I think. There are a lot of catalysts which really bring out these sorts of things.

SONG TITLE **Treat Me Right**

ARTIST Pat Benatar

Featured on Crimes of Passion. Released 1980/Chrysalis
Words & music by Pat Benatar

Pat Benatar (singer/songwriter):

The only problem I had with the women that were singing at the time was that they weren't doing the thing I wanted to do. I was looking for something else to do. Everybody was either part of a band or singing weepy songs. I didn't see any strength and that's what I wanted to do . . . I wanted to do a female version of what the bands that were fronted by men were doing.

SONG TITLE **Teach Your Children**

ARTIST Crosby, Stills, Nash and Young

Featured on Déjà Vu. Released 1970/Atlantic
Words & music by Graham Nash

Graham Nash (singer/songwriter):

The idea is that you write something so personal that every single person on the planet can relate to it. Once it's there on vinyl it unfolds, outwards, so that it applies to almost any situation. "Teach" started out as a slightly funky English folk song, but Stephen put a country beat to it and turned it into a hit record. Jerry Garcia added the pedal steel guitar—which he'd only been playing for two weeks.

SONG TITLE **Dreamboat Annie**

ARTIST Heart

Featured on Dreamboat Annie. Released 1976/Capitol
Words & music by Ann and Nancy Wilson

Nancy Wilson (singer/songwriter/guitarist):

We were searching for a title, and we were still recording. Ann just had the idea of calling it "Dreamboat Annie"—"Of course not about myself!" she says. Which is true, it's not really about Ann. It's about . . . a theme that comes up in a lot of our songs, like "Bebe Lestrange" and "Little Queen." It's a character that sort of grows up through our albums, which sort of represents us, but is not necessarily Ann or myself. But in many ways is—it's hard to explain.

SONG TITLE **Take Me to the Pilot**

ARTIST **Elton John**

Featured on Elton John. Released 1970/MCA
Words & music by Elton John and Bernie Taupin

Elton John (singer/songwriter):

I have no idea what that's about and neither does he [Bernie Taupin]!

Bernie Taupin (lyricist):

If anyone can tell me what the song is about—that would be great!

Love and Lust

Passion That Resulted in the Hits

Love and lust are the inspiration for hundreds of rock and roll songs. These two strong feelings have often been confused over the course of time. Songwriters are not immune to this confusion, on the contrary.

SONG TITLE **You Wear It Well**

ARTIST Rod Stewart

Featured on Never a Dull Moment. Released 1972/Mercury
Words & music by Rod Stewart and Martin Quittenton

Jo Jo Petrie:

Rod played it for me that June before my twenty-first birthday, both of us knowing without expressing it that our relationship had come to a bittersweet end. That last night we'd come back to the hotel after the show and Stewart was heading into the shower. He put on the record and coyly said, "I want you to hear this. You'll know what it means." . . . It still remains the most treasured gift I've ever received.

SONG TITLE **Don't Let the Sun Go Down on Me**

ARTIST Elton John

Featured on Caribou. Released 1974/MCA
Words & music by Elton John and Bernie Taupin

Gus Dudgeon (producer):

When Elton sang the vocal track, he was in a filthy mood. On some takes, he'd scream it, on others he'd mumble it. Or he'd just stand there, staring at the control room. Eventually, he flung off the cans and said, "Okay, let's hear what we got." When I played it to him, he said, "That's a load of fucking crap. You can send it to Engelbert Humperdinck, and if he doesn't like it, you can give it to Lulu as a demo."

SONG TITLE The Wind Cries Mary

ARTIST Jimi Hendrix

Featured on Are You Experienced? Released 1967/Reprise
Words & music by Jimi Hendrix

Kathy Mary Etchingham:

Jimi and I had a blistering row over my cooking. I got very angry and started throwing pots and pans and finally stormed out and went to stay with Angie and Eric [Burdon] for a day or so. When I did return, Jimi had written "The Wind Cries Mary" for me.

Jimi Hendrix (singer/songwriter/guitarist):

Mary's a girlfriend of mine, she tells the most nice stories to me. One time she tells me I'm an animal and another time she says I'm a kind of god to her. She is a girl who is slightly taking to talking about me to her friends, you know, one moment she will talk about me like a dog, and the next moment she says the complete opposite. But she is a nice girl underneath.

SONG TITLE **Follow You Follow Me**

ARTIST **Genesis**

Featured on And Then There Were Three . . .. Released 1978/Atlantic
Words & music by Tony Banks, Michael Rutherford and Phil Collins

Phil Collins (singer/songwriter/drummer):

It was just a rhythm riff of Mike's that we blew on and blew on for hours, and we tried it in different feels and different tempos. At one time it sounded really aggressive, but the one that sounded nice was when Mike slowed the riff down a bit, and I played this sort of Brazilian feel on it, and Tony put some chords behind and then we were doing it with just keyboards and guitar, with me singing, improvising a tune, and it was just a build up like that.

Mike Rutherford (songwriter/guitarist):

I consciously wrote simple lyrics. They really didn't say much, but they sound right for the song. They sound warm and friendly, which is unlike us really.

SONG TITLE **Maybe I'm Amazed**

ARTIST **Paul McCartney**

Featured on McCartney. Released 1970/Capitol
Words & music by Paul McCartney

Paul McCartney (singer/songwriter/instrumentalist):

When you're in love with someone—I mean, God it sounds soppy—but when you are in love and it's *new* like that, as it was for me and Linda with the Beatles breaking up, that was my feeling. Maybe I'm amazed at what's going on—maybe I'm not—but *maybe I am.* "Maybe I'm amazed at the way you pulled me out of time, hung me on the line." There were things that were happening at the time, and these phrases were my symbols for them. And other people seemed to understand.

SONG TITLE Miracles

ARTIST Jefferson Starship

Featured on Red Octopus. Released 1975/RCA
Words & music by Marty Balin

Marty Balin (singer/songwriter):

I like playing with eroticism and being very candid with people. But when you write something from deep inside, you have to go through the experience every time you sing it. The song forces you to. Onstage, I'll find myself going off, opening up into feelings, liberating myself. When the song is over, I'll wake up and see the audience really connected with me. Then I'll think, "Wow, I've done it."

I can't say the Starship enjoyed doing "Miracles." After we did the song, it was like my name was mud. I got a lot of criticism from within the band. It was very funny. Even now—I read a Starship interview just yesterday—Grace [Slick] is still putting me down for writing love songs and softening the band's sound. Yet what did Grace do when she first left the Starship? She made an album of mellow love songs.

SONG TITLE Misunderstanding

ARTIST Genesis

Featured on Duke. Released 1980/Atlantic
Words & music by Phil Collins

Phil Collins (singer/songwriter/drummer):

"Misunderstanding" was meant to be about a girl meeting a boy. It was meant to be a song that anybody could listen to—not just Genesis fans.

Tony Banks (songwriter/keyboardist):

I'm not that keen on "Misunderstanding." If it had never been brought out as a single, I'd probably like it better. But when you take it out of context and make it "The Single," in other words representing the whole album—which is what it was doing in the States—it just seemed rather insubstantial.

SONG TITLE **Our House**

ARTIST Crosby, Stills, Nash and Young

Featured on Déjà Vu. Released 1970/Atlantic
Words & music by Joni Mitchell

Joni Mitchell (singer/songwriter):

[It was] a little house, kind of a tree house. It was green, had a rural feeling to it, and was built into the side of a hill on Look Out Mountain Road. So when the trees spread out, the branches were right at the windows. Birds flew in and nested. It was a charmed little place, built by a black jazz piano player in the twenties as a weekend project. It had a kind of soulfulness and was full of knotty pine. [It] was hippie heaven, with a little rustic fireplace and a good feeling.

Graham Nash (singer/songwriter):

I felt very warm and felt like I'd really found a home . . . I had never been with a woman like Joan. I had never been so much in love.

SONG TITLE **Waiting For a Girl Like You**

ARTIST **Foreigner**

Featured on 4. Released 1981/Atlantic
Words & music by Mick Jones and Lou Gramm

Mick Jones (songwriter/guitarist):

"Waiting for a Girl Like You" dug down deep inside me. I really didn't know what was happening, but I had this feeling that something was guiding me to do it.

Lou Gramm (singer/songwriter):

Mick had played the intro and verse section for a number of weeks, and I found it to be really appealing. It had weight behind it, it wasn't a fragile groove. It did lack the chorus, which we eventually found. I had a rehearsal tape of Mick checking to see if the piano was in tune, and he played . . . [sings chorus melody] that part stuck with me and I saved this rehearsal tape and as we began to work on the song again I found that section and . . . it became the chorus of the song.

SONG TITLE You're in My Heart (The Final Acclaim)

ARTIST Rod Stewart

Featured on Foot Loose & Fancy Free. Released 1977/Warner Brothers
Words & music by Rod Stewart

Britt Ekland:

We went out to dinner with Billy Gaff and a bunch of friends one night to St. Germaine's, one of the poshest restaurants in Los Angeles. In the middle of the meal, Rod leaned over to me and whispered, "I've written a song for you" . . . No one took any notice as Rod softly sang the words into my ear. My eyes filled with tears. It was the loveliest song I had ever heard.

Rod Stewart (singer/songwriter):

It wasn't totally about Britt. The first verse could have been about Liz Treadwell. It could have been about anybody I met in that period—and there were a lot of them. It's a very confused song in a way. It's about a lot more than just women, it's also about my love of soccer. That's why my two favorite teams are mentioned at the end. The chorus is about Scotland. So it ends up being about three women, two football teams, and a country. And the line "You'll be my breath should I grow old"—I think that must have been about my mum and dad.

SONG TITLE Take It on the Run

ARTIST REO Speedwagon

Featured on Hi Infidelity. Released 1982/Epic
Words & music by Gary Richrath

Gary Richrath (guitarist/songwriter):

When I wrote that, I woke up one night, half asleep, and sat down in front of the TV. There was a soap opera on it. I was just sitting there, strumming a guitar, thinking: "God, these guys' relationships are worse than mine." I just sat there and sang vocals about the effects of gossip and relationships breaking up, which was what was on the tube and all that was similar to what was going on in my life.

SONG TITLE Poor, Poor Pitiful Me

ARTIST Linda Ronstadt

Featured on Simple Dreams. Released 1977/Asylum
Words & music by Warren Zevon

Linda Ronstadt (singer/songwriter):

I've never been into sadomasochism. I've never gotten that far out ever. To me that song seemed like the purest expression of male vanity. Step on you, be insensitive, be unkind, and give you a hard time saying, "Can't you take it, can't you take it!?" Then if you tease men in the slightest bit, they just walk off with their feelings hurt, stomp off in a corner, and pout. I mean that's the way men are. I swear. I thought the verse turned around to a female point of view was just perfect.

JOURNEY: members Neal Schon
and Steve Perry (Photo by Dave Lepori)

SONG TITLE Faithfully

ARTIST Journey

Featured on Frontiers. Released 1983/Columbia
Words & music by Jonathan Cain

Jonathan Cain (keyboardist/songwriter):

A song that's really special to me was a song I wrote on the road a couple years back, "Faithfully." I was feeling very alone, and I felt I needed to stay in a mood . . . a positive mood. I was on a bus before I wrote this and I had the vibrations of the wheels going around and it was all like in slow motion. What it describes best is the strength and the hope and the confidence that no matter what happens that you will remain faithful and the love for your lady will continue to grow and season even in the hardest conditions on the road.

SONG TITLE Piece of My Heart

ARTIST Janis Joplin

Featured on Janis Joplin's Greatest Hits. Released 1973/Columbia
Words & music by Bert Berns and Jerry Ragovoy

Country Joe McDonald (singer/songwriter):

She was a woman and she was a very feminine woman. I don't know what happened to her in Texas in her childhood, but I got the feeling that she was just the wrong person in the wrong place and got treated in the wrong way. She was real, she was a real woman.

SONG TITLE Don't You Want Somebody to Love

ARTIST the Jefferson Airplane

Featured on Surrealistic Pillow. Released 1967/RCA
Words and Music by Darby Slick

Darby Slick (songwriter):

I was living with Leslie. She was working at the post office, Rincon Annex, which, in those days was a haven for hippies and various intellectuals. Leslie loved rock and roll, but grew, by her statements, jealous of the attention I was receiving. One night I was home alone while she was working. I took some LSD and waited for her. She didn't come home. From hints she had dropped, which I hadn't understood, but had registered in my memory, I know that she wasn't injured, but was with someone else. At dawn, coming down from the drug, and miserable about our disintegrating relationship, I sat with my guitar and wrote: "When the truth is found to be lies / And all the joy within you dies / Don't you want somebody to love?" . . . The whole song came very quickly, words and music. I had no tape recorder, and didn't know how to write music notation, so I played it over and over, often sobbing as I tried to croak out the words. Finally, I went to sleep.

Grace Slick (singer/songwriter):

The sixties was a sensual revolution. We figured the whole thing was going to go on and on and more people were going to take acid, more of us were going to get enlightened. It wasn't like peace and love kinda stuff, it was, "Let's make music and screw around instead of making war." To a certain extent it was pretty arrogant and it was also the hedonism thing that said, "If you get in the way of my fun, fuck you."

SONG TITLE Can't Fight This Feeling

ARTIST REO Speedwagon

Featured on Wheels Are Turnin'. Released 1984/Epic
Words & music by Kevin Cronin

Kevin Cronin (singer/songwriter):

The band called it "the stupid ballad." It was supposed to be on the *Hi Infidelity* album, but I couldn't get the right lyrics. It was a song I'd been working on for a long time . . . so I talked to Billy Steinberg and Tom Kelly [songwriters]. So we sat down at the piano—it will come out if it's in there—and before I knew it the song was finished.

SONG TITLE Hello, I Love You

ARTIST the Doors

Featured on Waiting for the Sun. Released 1968/Elektra
Words & music by Jim Morrison, Robbie Krieger, John Densmore and Ray Manzarek

Jim Morrison (singer/songwriter):

Actually, I think the music came to my mind first and then I made up the words to hang on to the melody, some kind of sound. I could hear it, and since I had no way of writing it down musically, the only way I could remember it was to try and get words to put to it. And a lot of times I would end up with just the words and couldn't remember the melody.

SONG TITLE **Little Wing**

ARTIST **Jimi Hendrix**

Featured on Axis: Bold as Love. Released 1967/Reprise
Words & music by Jimi Hendrix

Jimi Hendrix (singer/songwriter/guitarist):

I see nothing but gypsy people on the road. And gypsy is America today, the new and the live America. You say, "Why do you call yourself that? Why don't you get a strong name?" Forget about . . . we have to relate. You have to give 'em a name that they know, you know. So like "Little Wing" is like one of these beautiful girls that come around sometimes. They might be spaced. They might be, you know—kind of strung out on a certain this or that. You know everybody has a right to their own releases or their own beliefs, if they want to believe that a star is purple or whatever. And like these girls, which is one girl to me, it's like "The Wind Cries Mary" is representing more than one person. And like she's the one that really comes around. Put it in another picture. You ride in town; the war happens. You ride in town for the drinks and parties and so forth. You play your gig; it's the same thing as the olden days. And these beautiful girls come around and really entertain you. You do actually fall in love with them because that's the only love you can have. It's not always the physical thing of "Oh, there's one over there . . ." It's not one of those scenes. They actually tell you something. They release different things inside themselves, and then you feel to yourself, "Damn, there's really a responsibility to some of these girls, you know, because they're the ones that are gonna get screwed" . . . "Little Wing" was a very sweet girl that came around that gave me her whole life and more if I wanted it. And me with my crazy ass couldn't get it together, so I'm off here and there and off over there.

SONG TITLE Night Moves

ARTIST Bob Seger

Featured on Night Moves. Released 1976/Capitol
Words & music by Bob Seger

Bob Seger (singer/songwriter):

I was shy, super shy. And I happened to fall into a faster crowd than I'd ever been in before. Because I played music, I was sort of a gimmick for those guys. And I got to meet the really "hot" chicks and I had my first great love affair, which is really what "Night Moves" is about, it's about that girl. You know, the girl with the big breasts that we all went kazappo for when we reached puberty. It was a really mad, crazy affair.

The album as well as the song was inspired by *American Graffiti.* I came out of the theater thinking, "Hey, I've got a story to tell, too! Nobody has ever told about how it was to grow up in my neck of the woods."

SONG TITLE Slow Ride

ARTIST Foghat

Featured on Fool for the City. Released 1975/Bearsville
Words & music by Dave Peverett

Dave Peverett (singer/songwriter/guitarist):

"Slow Ride" was not a sellout—it's just us. We didn't go AM to get a hit 45. But "Slow Ride" did add a whole lot of new faces, young faces, to the show audiences . . .

Roger Price (guitarist):

Even if they don't understand what "Slow Ride" is about!

SONG TITLE **Young Lust**

ARTIST Pink Floyd

Featured on The Wall. Released 1979/Columbia
Words & music by Roger Waters and David Gilmour

Roger Waters (singer/songwriter):

When I wrote the song "Young Lust," the words were all quite different. It was about leaving school and wandering town and hanging around outside porno movies and dirty bookshops and being very interested in sex, but never actually being able to get involved because of being too frightened. Now it's completely different, that was a function of us all working together on the record, particularly with Dave Gilmour and Bob Ezrin—we coproduced the album together. "Young Lust" is a pastiche . . . of any young rock and roll band out on the road.

SONG TITLE **Woman from Tokyo**

ARTIST Deep Purple

Featured on Who Do We Think We Are. Released 1973/Warner Brothers
Words & music by Ritchie Blackmore, Jon Lond, Ian Gillan, Roger Glover and Ian Paice

Roger Glover (bassist):

We wrote this song before we left for Japan in August. It's all about a chick in Tokyo, and I guess you could say we were fantasizing about what it would be like over there. But the funny thing about it is that it really came true. I met a girl over in Japan, and now I do have a Japanese girlfriend.

SONG TITLE **Still . . . You Turn Me On**

ARTIST Emerson, Lake and Palmer

Featured on Brain Salad Surgery. Released 1973/Atlantic
Words & music by Greg Lake

Carl Palmer (drummer):

We've had success through Greg's ballads. Without those we probably wouldn't have sold the amount of records that we have. The problem was when we had something which was a commercial hit, it wasn't dark. We had love songs that were hits, so it was a rather diverse situation; people were always waiting for the next "C'est La Vie," "Lucky Man," "Still . . . You Turn Me On," or "From the Beginning."

SONG TITLE **Love the One You're With**

ARTIST Stephen Stills

Featured on Stephen Stills. Released 1970/Atlantic
Words & music by Stephen Stills

Stephen Stills (singer/songwriter/guitarist):

This song has been very good to me. The title came from a party with Billy Preston. I asked him if I could pinch this line he had, and he said, "Sure." So I took the phrase and wrote a song around it. It's a good times song, just a bit of fun.

SONG TITLE Ready For Love

ARTIST Bad Company

Featured on Bad Company. Released 1974/Swan Song
Words & music by Mick Ralphs

Paul Rodgers (singer/songwriter):

I don't like lyrics to be overbearing. I like them to say something. But I'm not trying to change the world overnight. Something simple and understandable that people can relate their own everyday experiences to. Mick also writes the same way. We do a song that's been knocking around for years called "Ready for Love." They played it in Mott [the Hopple], but we treat it completely differently—more like a heavy ballad. We play the number as we hear it, rather than trying to make it more than it is. It's very mellow, and we do it at a speed where I can get the words over, so they're not rushed. I always try to write lyrics I can actually speak. Like if I'm talking to a chick, then I'd want to say certain things without any embarrassment. It has to be simple.

SONG TITLE Do Ya Think I'm Sexy?

ARTIST Rod Stewart

Featured on Blondes Have More Fun. Released 1978/Warner Brothers
Words & music by Rod Stewart and Carmen Appice

Rod Stewart (singer/songwriter):

Isn't it a wonder I've survived some of my fucking terrible career moves? Sometimes I worry about me! "Do Ya Think I'm Sexy?" If I was a male fan, I'd think, "Up yours, Jack!"

Protest Songs

Rock 'n' Roll at Its Rebellious Best

Rock and roll has always been about rebellion. It was supposed to be the loud, defiant music your parents would hate (although with the baby boomers reaching their fifties this has become more difficult). Occasionally a songwriter would set their sights on a worthy target for their anger and venom.

SONG TITLE **Another Brick in the Wall (Part Two)**

ARTIST Pink Floyd

Featured on The Wall. Released 1979/Columbia
Words & music by Roger Waters

Roger Waters (singer/songwriter):

When I hear people whining on now about bringing back grammar schools, it really makes me quite ill to listen to it. Because I went to a boys grammar school, and although . . . I want to make it plain that some of the men who taught there were very nice guys, you know I'm not . . . it's not meant to be a blanket condemnation of teachers everywhere, but the bad ones can really do people in—and there were some at my school who were just incredibly bad and treated the children so badly, just putting them down . . . all the time. Never encouraging them to do things, not really trying to interest them in anything, just trying to keep them quiet and still, and crush them into the right shape, so that they would go to university and "do well."

SONG TITLE **Fortunate Son**

ARTIST Creedence Clearwater Revival

Featured on Willy & the Poor Boys. Released 1969/Fantasy
Words & music by John Fogerty

John Fogerty (singer/songwriter/guitarist):

It was written, of course, during the Nixon era, and well, let's say I was very nonsupportive of Mr. Nixon. There just seemed to be this trickle down to the offspring of people like him. I remember you would hear about Tricia Nixon and David Eisenhower. . . . You got the impression that these people got preferential treatment, and the whole idea of being born wealthy or being born powerful seemed to really be coming to the fore in the late-sixties confrontation of cultures.

SONG TITLE **For What It's Worth**

ARTIST **Buffalo Springfield**

Featured on Buffalo Springfield. Released 1967/Atco
Words & music by Stephen Stills

Stephen Stills (singer/songwriter/guitarist):

I'd just come from Latin America after being caught in Nicaragua . . . when I saw the Sunset Strip riots . . . all the kids on one side of the street, all the cops on the other side. In Latin America, that meant there would be a new government in about a week.

David Crosby (singer/songwriter):

I remember him going [imitating the opening guitar harmonics] "brrrang, bump, ba, de, da, brrrang . . . And I told him, "That's a great lick, man." Stephen said, "Oh? You really think so? It's part of this new song I've got going called "For What It's Worth."

SONG TITLE Jumpin' Jack Flash

ARTIST the Rolling Stones

Featured on Hot Rocks. Released 1972/ABKCO
Words & music by Mick Jagger and Keith Richards

Keith Richards (songwriter/guitarist):

As soon as I pick up the guitar and play that "Jumpin' Jack Flash" riff, something happens here—in your stomach. It's one of the better feelings in the world. You just jump on the riff, and it plays you. Matter of fact, it takes you over. An explosion would be the best way to describe it. It's the one that I would immediately go to if I wanted to approach the state of nirvana. Maybe that's what this entire generation felt. An explosion. A rebellion against boredom, and conformity. That's why it broke out amongst white kids like me. Suddenly something happened: Its first impact was an invasion. Like the barbarians at the gates of Rome.

SONG TITLE Ohio

ARTIST by Crosby, Stills, Nash and Young

Featured on So Far. Released 1974/Atlantic
Words & music by Neil Young

Neil Young (singer/songwriter/guitarist):

I had the *Time* magazine there, with that girl looking up from a dead student lying on the ground with the blood and the whole deal. I just wrote it. It just came out right there on the porch. It was really like the folk process at work. You know, that was really like music as news.

David Crosby (singer/songwriter):

Neil surprised everybody. It wasn't like he set out as a project to write a protest song. It's just what came out of having *Huntley-Brinkley* for breakfast.

Neil Young:

It's still hard to believe I had to write this song. It's ironic that I capitalized on the deaths of these American students. Probably the biggest lesson ever learned at an American place of learning. My best CSN&Y cut.

Graham Nash (singer/songwriter):

What band would have a song like "Teach Your Children" racing up the charts and then immediately kill it stone dead when four students were killed? Neil wrote "Ohio," and we recorded it and put it out within ten days. People in the business thought we were absolutely crazy.

SONG TITLE **Revolution**

ARTIST the Beatles

Featured on The Beatles ("the White Album"). Released 1968/Capitol
Words & music by Paul McCartney and John Lennon

John Lennon (singer/songwriter):

The underground left only picked up on the [single version] that said, "count me out." The original version which ends up on the LP said "count me in" too; I put in both because I wasn't sure . . . On the version released as a single I said, "When you talk about destruction you can count me out." I didn't want to get killed.

SONG TITLE **School's Out**

ARTIST Alice Cooper

Featured on School's Out. Released 1972/Warner Brothers
Words & music by Alice Cooper and Michael Bruce

Alice Cooper (singer/songwriter):

What's the difference between being locked up in school and being locked up in jail. . . . I had a column on the Cortez High School paper called "Get Outta My Hair." I always signed it Muscles McNasal because I was skinny and had a great big nose. I got kicked out eight times in 64 days even though my hair wasn't that long. . . . I'd love to go back and visit Cortez High School; but needless to say, I didn't get invited to the reunion.

SONG TITLE **The Times They Are A-Changin'**

ARTIST Bob Dylan

Featured on The Times They Are A-Changin'. Released 1964/Columbia
Words & music by Bob Dylan

Bob Dylan (singer/songwriter):

This was definitely a song with a purpose. I knew exactly what I wanted to say and for whom I wanted to say it. I wanted to write a big song, some kind of theme song, you know, with short concise verses that piled up on each other in a hypnotic way.

SONG TITLE **Who'll Stop the Rain?**

ARTIST Creedence Clearwater Revival

Featured on Cosmo's Factory. Released 1970/Fantasy
Words & music by John Fogerty

John Fogerty (singer/songwriter/guitarist):

Protest songs were always kind of done with a real loud approach vocally and a harmonica à la Bob Dylan. I really wanted to do a song about the times [the Vietnam War], but I didn't want to be obvious. I wanted to say what I wanted to say and come to people in layers, so they were absorbing the beauty of it and enjoying the song, before it ever occurred to them what it was actually about.

WHO, The: members Keith Moon,
Roger Daltrey, and Pete Townshend
(Photo by Anastasia Pantsios)

SONG TITLE Won't Get Fooled Again

ARTIST the Who

Featured on Who's Next. Released 1971/MCA
Words & music by Peter Townshend

Peter Townshend (singer/songwriter/guitarist):

It's really a bit of a weird song. The first verse sounds like a revolution song, and the second like somebody getting tired of it. Basically, it's the same vein as "We're Not Gonna Take It" [from *Tommy*]. It's an angry antiestablishment song. It's anti-people who are negative. A song against the revolution because the revolution is only a revolution, and a revolution is not going to change anything at all in the long run, and a lot of people are going to get hurt. When I wrote "We're Not Gonna Take It," it was really we're not gonna take fascism. "Won't Get Fooled Again" I wrote at a time when I was getting barraged by people at the Eel Pie island commune. They live opposite me. There was like a love affair going on between me and them. . . . They dug me because I was like a figurehead . . . in a group . . . and I dug them because I could see what was going on over there. At one point there was an amazing scene where the commune was really working, but then the acid started flowing and I got on the end of some psychotic conversations. And I just thought "Oh, fuck it."

SONG TITLE **Hell Is For Children**

ARTIST Pat Benatar

Featured on Crimes of Passion. Released 1980/Chrysalis
Words & music by Neil Geraldo, Pat Benatar and Roger Capps

Pat Benatar (singer/songwriter):

I started writing this with Roger Capps, our old bass player, because I had read this huge article in the *New York Times.* It was a serial article that went on for a couple of weeks. I came from a really small town, and if anyone was ever abused you certainly never heard about it. I had no idea to what extent it had gotten so out of hand in the country. This article was a bombardment of statistics and gruesome accounts, cases and convictions. . . . It was such saturation that by the time the week was over I was devastated. I had no idea that this was going on, and for some reason it became my pet thing from that time on. So Roger and I started to write that song—we had these lyrics and we didn't know what to do with them, because we thought it was too heavy . . . we wanted to make it into a viable rock song . . . I told Neil [Geraldo] that I wanted it to sound like pain. So that's why that screaming is in there, because he just wrote it so it would sound like pain. And every night when I do it, that's the motivation behind it. It's so you can hear the agony, whatever they're going through—that was the point of that chorus.

SONG TITLE Yours Is No Disgrace

ARTIST Yes

Featured on The Yes Album. Released 1971/Atlantic
Words & music by Jon Anderson, Chris Squire, Steve Howe, Bill Bruford and Tony Kaye

Jon Anderson (singer/songwriter):

It was Vietnam at the time, and kids were going out there that had to fight, and it's not their fault they had to fight. They had to get into it. They had to get on top of it or else they were going to get killed. They had to get on top of the whole situation. And that's what struck me, that it wasn't a disgrace to fight, even though the innermost feelings of man is that it's the most cruel, degrading, abysmal thing to be doing is to kill your fellow man.

SONG TITLE Street Fighting Man

ARTIST the Rolling Stones

Featured on Beggars Banquet. Released 1968/ABKCO
Words & music by Mick Jagger and Keith Richards

Mick Jagger (singer/songwriter):

That was during that radical Vietnam time. It was merely then. You've always got to have good tunes if you're marching. But the tunes didn't make the march. Basically, rock and roll isn't protest, and never was. It's not political. It's only—it promotes interfamilial tension. It used to. Now it can't even do that, because fathers don't ever get outraged with the music. Either they like it, or it sounds similar to what they liked as kids. So rock and roll's gone, that's all gone.

Writing a Stairway to Heaven

The Greatest Rock Anthems

Most of the major classic rock artists have one song that they are indelibly associated with and that practically anyone would recognize. These are the songs that are played endlessly on the FM dial and are usually saved for the encore of the band's show. Quite often the song will turn into a kind of albatross around their necks and for their hard-core fans who have heard it more times than they care to remember. Yet the reason these songs are so enduring is that they are genuinely inspired pieces of music . . . .

SONG TITLE Aqualung

ARTIST Jethro Tull

Featured on Aqualung. Released 1971/Chrysalis
Words & music by Ian and Jennie Anderson

Ian Anderson (singer/songwriter/instrumentalist):

I was very briefly married at the time, and when we got married, neither she nor I wanted her to play the role of the faithful housewife, but we thought she should study something or do something. . . . She decided she wanted to take up and study photography. So she went off to college to do that.

One of the first assignments she had was to record images of homeless people—vagrants—living in cardboard boxes in a certain part of London. And she came back with some photographs that she'd taken and developed. I think she had scribbled a few lines on the back of one of the prints, or on an accompanying piece of paper, with lines describing this guy. I hadn't seen the person; I had only seen the photograph. In trying to encompass something that was just a black-and-white image—just a grainy, Kodak Tri-X student photographer image—there was a certain degree of detachment that led me to romanticize the character, and add to her few words.

It just developed into a song—the first verse, "Sun streaking cold, an old man wandering lonely . . . " is the bit I think was my first wife's contribution. But the introductory, heavy-riff bit almost certainly is a musical idea of mine with a lyric that ties in.

Take a person, one who is very lowly, right at the bottom like the tramp in the song. Well, there is still within such a man as much of God as there is in the pope. I guess it's a song about spiritual equality, and that is what the rest of the songs are about too—spiritual equality, looking for God in man, any man.

Martin Barre (guitarist):

Ian wrote all of it inasmuch as he wrote the riff and the verses. The form was just verse riff, and he had the lyrics. We needed a guitar solo, so I said, "Why don't we just base it on the chords of the verse, but break it down into half time, then do a sort of round sequence to do a solo over?" And it worked well. While I was doing the solo, which was going really well, Jimmy Page walked into the control room and started waving. I thought, "Should I wave back and mess up the solo or should I just grin and carry on?" Being a professional to the end, I just grinned.

SONG TITLE **Back in Black**

ARTIST AC/DC

Featured on Back in Black. Released 1980/Atco
Words & music by Malcolm Young and Brian Johnson

Angus Young (guitarist):

Malcolm [had the main riff for] "Back in Black" for about three weeks. He came in one night and said, "You got your cassette here? Can I put this down? It's driving me mad. I won't be getting any sleep until I put it on cassette." The funniest thing is he said to me, "What do you think? I don't know if it's crap or not, I don't know."

Brian Johnson (singer/songwriter):

I don't think anybody writing lyrics could miss with those riffs. You could have written anything, and it would have sounded good. I think it was professionals meeting up with a rank amateur myself, and it just meshed. Just an accident. Just an amateur who thought, "Well, I'd better write these quick." The professionals had the gears oiled, and it all just fit perfectly.

SONG TITLE **Black Magic Woman**

ARTIST **Santana**

Featured on Abraxas. Released 1970/Columbia
Words & music by Peter Green

Carlos Santana (songwriter/guitarist):

We decided to record it after Greg Rolie, the keyboard player and singer at the time, started playing it at a sound check in Fresno. If you listen to Fleetwood Mac's, it's very different than ours, even though it's the same song. We arranged it differently and put our own fingerprints on it, and it became our "Black Magic Woman" even though they get the royalties.

SONG TITLE **Blinded by the Light**

ARTIST **Manfred Mann**

Featured on The Roaring Silence. Released 1976/Warner Brothers
Words & music by Bruce Springsteen

Manfred Mann (singer/songwriter/keyboardist):

I thought perhaps that something could be done with "Blinded." But I worked on it a lot, and there were a lot of problems in doing it. Even the original arrangement [by Bruce Springsteen] was quite hard, because it builds up through the verses. . . . It didn't come out as I originally imagined . . . for a while I was unhappy with it.

SONG TITLE **Bohemian Rhapsody**

ARTIST **Queen**

Featured on A Night at the Opera. Released 1975/Hollywood (rerelease)
Words & music by Freddie Mercury

Freddie Mercury (singer/songwriter):

A lot of people slammed "Bohemian Rhapsody," but who can you compare that to? Name one group that's done an operatic single. You know, we were adamant that it would be a hit in its entirety. We have been forced to make compromises, but cutting up a song will never be one of them.

Roy Thomas Baker (producer):

It wasn't all recorded in one go. We did the whole of the first section and the rock section, and for the middle part, we just hit some drums now and then, after which it was basically edits—we just lengthened the middle section depending on what vocals were put in, because Freddie would come up with amazing ideas. He'd walk in and say "I've got some new ideas for the vocals—we'll stick some Galileos in here . . . ." I'd say that track, on its own, took getting on for three weeks.

SONG TITLE Born to Run

ARTIST Bruce Springsteen

Featured on Born to Run. Released 1975/Columbia
Words & music by Bruce Springsteen

Bruce Springsteen (singer/songwriter/guitarist):

"Born to Run" was about New York. I was there for months. I had this girl with me and she'd come in from Texas and she wanted to go home again. And she was going nuts and we were in this room and it just went on and on. I'd come home practically in tears. And I was sort of into that whole thing of being nowhere. But knowing there is something someplace.

Mike Appel (manager):

When I came back to the office after the initial play of the song for CBS, Bruce asked me what they thought of it. "Not much," I told him. "What are we going to do now?" he asked. I sat down and said, "Well, what are our options? You just brought 'Born to Run' to the record company, and nobody seems to like it a whole lot."

We were getting pretty desperate. I mean, six months' work on a single that nobody at the record company liked! How was I ever going to move this monstrous record label, whose support was still solidly behind acts like Chicago, Barbra Streisand, Neil Diamond, Billy Joel, and now even Aerosmith, but certainly not Bruce Springsteen. I suggested we take the tape directly to some deejays we'd built good relationships with—guys like Kid Leo in Cleveland, Ed Sciaky in Philadelphia, some guys in Phoenix, a couple in Boston.

There were about 33 stations in some pretty big markets that went on the tape of "Born to Run" as soon as I sent it to them. We made up about 40 copies onto cassettes, so now the song was two generations down from the normal broadcast quality, but it didn't seem to matter. "Born to Run" went to number one in Cleveland immediately, based solely on airplay.

Now people were coming into the stores—in Cleveland, Dallas, Boston, all over—looking for the new Springsteen album, which didn't exist. All we'd cut to that point was a single which hadn't been released. Well, CBS went totally out of its collective corporate mind. In their eyes we'd created the sin of sins, pissing away valuable airplay without having any product in the store to sell. Nothing. CBS wanted to take me into the street and kick my skinny little ass all over this town. They would have strangled me if they could have. I'd broken rank in the chain of command, and that was just untenable to the guys upstairs.

SONG TITLE **Born to Be Wild**

ARTIST Steppenwolf

Featured on Steppenwolf. Released 1974/MCA
Words & music by Dennis Edmonton

Dennis Edmonton (songwriter):
I was walking down Hollywood Boulevard one day and saw a poster in a window saying "Born to Ride" with a picture of a motorcycle erupting out of the earth like a volcano with all this fire around it. Around this time I had just purchased my first car, a little secondhand Ford Falcon. So all this came together lyrically: the idea of the motorcycle coming out along with the freedom and joy I felt in having my first car and being able to drive myself around whenever I wanted . . . . "Born to Be Wild" didn't stand out initially. Even the publishers at Leeds Music didn't take it as the first or second song I gave them. They got it only because I signed as a staff writer. Luckily, it stood out for Steppenwolf. It's like a fluke rather than an achievement, though.

SONG TITLE **Carry On Wayward Son**

ARTIST **Kansas**

Featured on Leftoverture. Released 1976/Kirshner
Words & music by Kerry Livgren

Kerry Livgren (songwriter/guitarist):

I wrote "Carry On" the next to last day of rehearsal before we went in the studio. We were not supposed to be bringing up new songs. At that point, we were only supposed to be coming up with the final touches on the ones that we had chosen. I walked into rehearsal and said, "I've got one more song that you might want to hear." Everybody said, "Hey, that's kind of neat. Maybe we ought to learn it and take it into the studio and see what it sounds like." By the time we got into the studio and recorded it with the a cappella vocals, everybody said it should be the opening cut. I don't know why it was so successful; I really don't have any idea, it was just the right time.

My goal was inaccessible, but I felt a profound urge to "carry on" and continue the search. I saw myself as the "wayward son," alienated from the ultimate reality, and yet striving to know it or him. The positive note at the end ("Now your life's no longer empty/Surely heaven waits for you") seemed strange and premature, but I felt impelled to include it in the lyrics. It proved to be prophetic.

SONG TITLE Dream On

ARTIST Aerosmith

Featured on Aerosmith. Released 1973/Columbia
Words & music by Steven Tyler

Steven Tyler (singer/songwriter):

This song sums up the shit you put up with when you're in a new band. Only one in fifty people who write about you pick on the music. Most of the critics panned our first album, and said we were ripping off the Stones. And I think "Dream On" is a great song, but it was two or three years before people really got a chance to hear it. That's a good barometer of my anger at the press, which I still have. "Dream On" came of me playing the piano when I was about seventeen or eighteen, and I didn't know anything about writing a song. It was just this little . . . sonnet that I started playing one day. I never thought that it would end up being a real song or anything.

SONG TITLE Frankenstein

ARTIST The Edgar Winter Group

Featured on They Only Come Out at Night. Released 1972/Epic
Music by Edgar Winter

Rick Derringer (producer):

Edgar wrote this song called "The Double Drum Solo," just for a working name, and every night when he came out he'd bring down the house. At the end of the song he'd get to play sax, he'd get to play keyboards, he'd get to play drums—he'd get to play everything.

When it came time for Edgar to do his first band album, *They Only Come Out at Night,* he wanted to include that instrumental in the album. Bill Szymczyk and I—I was the producer and he was the engineer—were really looking forward to doing that song. To us, we're musicians, the rest of the album was a little more predictable. The one thing that seemed like it was going to be fun was the instrumental. At one point in the project, Edgar started to be nervous. "Oh, I don't know, it's a little too crazy. Is this gonna be too jazzy, too out of context for the rest of the album?" All of us voiced our opinions immediately, saying, "It's fantastic, it's gotta be on the record." We went ahead and finished it; we did some editing to shorten it, as it was too long in the live form. The editing is where Edgar got the name "Frankenstein," through all the little cuts and stuff, all the patches in [the] master.

SONG TITLE **Free Bird**

ARTIST Lynyrd Skynyrd

Featured on (pronounced leh-nerd skin-nerd). Released 1973/MCA
Words & music by Allen Collins and Ronnie Van Zant

Gary Rossington (guitarist):

It was a slow song, and it ended too early. We were doing four sets a night, and Ronnie said we needed to make the song longer, because we didn't have enough material and were trying not to do any covers. Each night the song got a little longer, but Ronnie always said to make it longer. Finally, it was ten minutes long.

Ed King (guitarist):

MCA said we couldn't put a ten-minute song on an album, because nobody would play it. Of course, that was the song everyone gravitated towards!

SONG TITLE **Gimme Some Lovin'**

ARTIST the Spencer Davis Group

Featured on The Golden Archive Series (repackaged). Released 1984/Rhino
Words & music by Steve Winwood, Muff Winwood and Spencer Davis

Spencer Davis (guitarist):

"Gimme Some Lovin' " was written with an American perspective. We used to rehearse at the Marquee Club in London, and Muff had a bass riff from an old record by Homer Banks called "Whole Lotta Lovin'." I hadn't heard that song, but I thought the riff Muff was playing was fantastic. I added a G, A, and a C minor to it, Steve played a Ravel's "Bolero" kind of thing, and Steve said to me, "Don't play major, play minors."

The English version was a stark, haunting thing, but the American version, which everybody knows best, had backing vocals. It was number two in England, and the only thing that kept it from number one was "Good Vibrations" by the Beach Boys. Steve and us had just the sound America craved!

SONG TITLE **Heart of Gold**

ARTIST Neil Young

Featured on Harvest. Released 1972/Reprise
Words & music by Neil Young

Neil Young (singer/songwriter/guitarist):

I realized I had a long way to go and this wasn't going to be the most satisfying thing, just sitting around basking in the glory of having a hit record. It's really a very shallow experience.

This song puts me in the middle of the road. Traveling there became a bore, so I headed for the ditch. A rougher ride, but I saw more interesting people there.

SONG TITLE **In-a-Gadda-Da-Vida**

ARTIST Iron Butterfly

Featured on In-a-Gadda-Da-Vida. Released 1968/Atco
Words & music by Doug Ingle

Ron Bushy (drummer):

I came home one night and found Doug. He had been working on a song and polished off the whole gallon of Red Mountain wine. What he had been working on was this thing called "In the Garden of Eden," but he was so drunk that when he sang it to me he slurred the words into "In-a-Gadda-Da-Vida." I thought it sounded real clever and wrote it down exactly, and it stuck.

SONG TITLE **Iron Man**

ARTIST Black Sabbath

Featured on Paranoid. Released 1971/Warner Brothers
Words & music by Tony Iommi, Ozzy Osbourne, Geezer Butler and Bill Ward

Tony Iommi (guitarist/songwriter):

The "Iron Man" riffs were basically done without vocals because Ozzy would follow the riff . . . one of the reasons riffs developed was to keep the audience quiet. If everybody was talking during the gig, we cranked it up to get their attention.

Ozzy Osbourne (singer/songwriter):

I wish I didn't have to perform "Iron Man" every night.

SONG TITLE **The Joker**

ARTIST the Steve Miller Band

Featured on The Joker. Released 1973/Capitol
Words & music by Steve Miller

Steve Miller (singer/songwriter/guitarist):

I never thought it was going to be a hit. I took the challenge; I said, "Okay, it's got to be two-and-a-half minutes long, and it's got to follow a soul-disco symphony." I always wanted to make singles; I like singles . . . . So I just started taking that two-and-a-half-minute thing and started looking for sounds that record well . . . . It's like a game, like a crossword puzzle. And as long as you get some tunes that have got feeling and soul and substance to them, there you go.

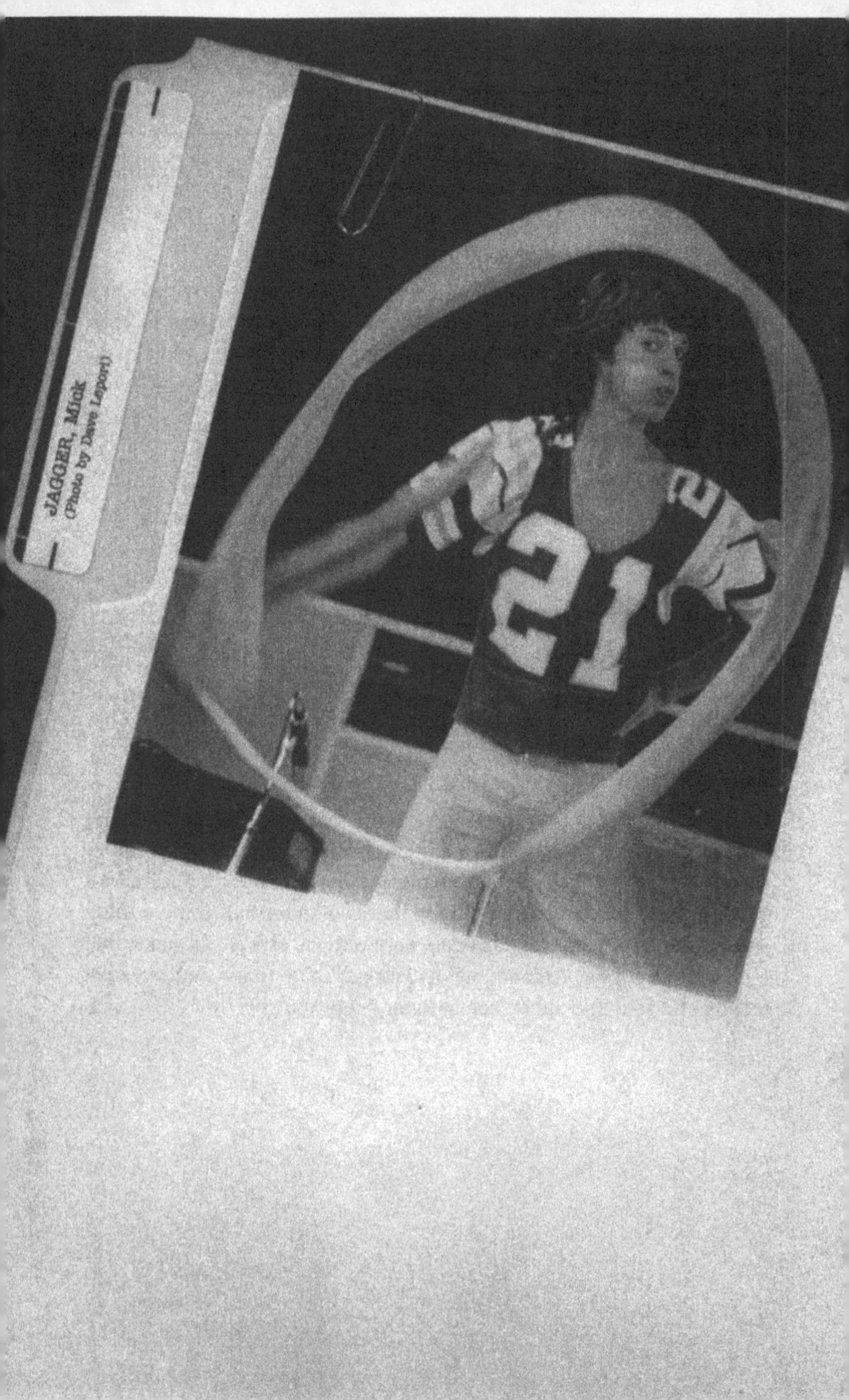
JAGGER, Mick
(Photo by Dave Lepori)

SONG TITLE Jumpin' Jack Flash

ARTIST the Rolling Stones

Featured on Hot Rocks. Released 1972/ABKCO
Words & music by Mick Jagger and Keith Richards

Keith Richards (songwriter/guitarist):

Mick and I were in my house down in the south of England. It was about six in the morning. The sky was just beginning to go gray. It was pissing down rain, if I remember rightly. "Jumpin' Jack Flash" comes from this guy Jack Dyer, who was my gardener. He'd lived in the country all his life. I'll put it this way: Jack Dyer, an old English yokel.

. . . So Mick and I were sitting there. And suddenly Mick starts up. He hears these great footsteps, these big rubber boots—slosh, slosh, slosh—going by the window. He said, "What's that?" And I said, "Oh, that's Jack. That's jumpin' Jack." And we had the open tuning on my guitar. I started to fool around with that [singing] "Jumpin' Jack." And Mick says, "Flash." He'd just woken up. And suddenly we had this wonderful alliterative phrase.

SONG TITLE Karn Evil 9 1st Impression (Part Two)

ARTIST Emerson, Lake and Palmer

Featured on Brain Salad Surgery. Released 1973/Atlantic
Words & music by Keith Emerson, Greg Lake and Pete Sinfield

Keith Emerson (songwriter/keyboardist):

I had this idea about a planet that I wanted to call "Ganton 9." And Pete [Sinfield, lyricist] said you can't call it that, 'cause there's a Ganton Street in Soho, just down the road! Pete listened to the music I'd written and said it sounds like a carnival—it's all happy! So we went carnival, hmm, Karn Evil. Bang! That's it—end of story!

Peter Sinfield:

[Tom] Lehrer is a big hero of mine, and I can hear little bits of Lehrer and pieces of Vonnegut and other things that I've absorbed along the way. The best bit in it is "Welcome back, my friends, to the show that never ends . . ." which ELP of course used for years.

SONG TITLE **Layla**

ARTIST **Derek and the Dominoes**

Featured on Layla & Other Assorted Love Songs. Released 1970/Polydor
Words & music by Eric Clapton and James Beck Gordon

Eric Clapton (singer/songwriter/guitarist):

It was actually about an emotional experience, a woman that I felt deeply about and who turned me down, and I had to kind of pour it out in some way . . . her husband [George Harrison] is a great musician. It's the wife-of-my-best-friend scene, and her husband has been writing great songs for years about her, and she still left him. You see, he grabbed one of my chicks, and so I thought I'd get even with him one day, on a petty level, and it grew from that. She was trying to attract his attention, and so she used me, and I fell madly in love with her. If you listen to the words of "Layla": "I tried to give you consolation / When your old man had let you down / Like a fool, I fell in love with you / You turned my whole world upside down."

The greatest things you do are always done by mistake, accidentally. I had no idea what "Layla" was going to be. It was just a ditty. When you get near to the end of it, that's when your enthusiasm starts building, and you know you've got something really powerful. You can be so-so about it as you're making the track, singing the vocals, but if, as you start to add stuff and mix it, it becomes gross, then you really are in charge of something powerful. What I'm saying is, when I started to do that, it didn't feel like anything special to me.

SONG TITLE Light My Fire

ARTIST the Doors

Featured on The Doors. Released 1967/Elektra
Words & music by Robby Krieger

Robby Krieger (guitarist/songwriter):
In order to compete with Jim's songs, I knew I'd have to be pretty good. I figured I'd keep it on a universal scale and write about earth, air, fire, or water. I picked fire, mainly because I always liked that song by the Stones, "Play with Fire."

Ray Manzarek (keyboardist):
Jim objected to doing "Light My Fire." He had to do it the same way every night, but we got to stretch out for 15 or 20 minutes—however long we wanted for our solos. We would do Indian improvisations, we would trade fours and twos and ones with John, anything. And Morrison, unfortunately, had to do the same thing "You know that it would be untrue . . ." There was nothing he could do about it.

SONG TITLE Lights

ARTIST Journey

Featured on Infinity. Released 1978/Columbia
Words & music by Steve Perry and Neil Schon

Steve Perry (singer/songwriter):

[The song was originally inspired] because I was overlooking the city of Los Angeles one time from Griffith Park, and it was really early in the morning. It was started probably a year before I joined Journey; it was sort of sitting in the back of my mind . . . . When Journey called me, that was probably the second song we worked up after "Patiently." Neil helped me finish it and because the group was from San Francisco, I started thinking about it—we spent many nights coming across that bay at sunrise—for obvious reasons! It was crazy, those days were crazy. The song just sort of popped out and sort of finished itself. It was probably meant to be about San Francisco and that sunrise as city lights go down.

SONG TITLE Like a Rolling Stone

ARTIST Bob Dylan

Featured on Highway 61 Revisited. Released 1965/Columbia
Words & music by Bob Dylan

Bob Dylan (singer/songwriter):

The chorus part came to me first, and I'd sorta hum that over and over. Then I later figured out that the verses would start low and move up. The first two lines, which rhymed "kiddin' you" with "didn't you," just about knocked me out; and later on when I got to the jugglers and the chrome horse and the princess on the steeple, it all just about got to be too much.

I'd literally quit singing and playing and I found myself writing this song, this story, this long piece of vomit, about 20 pages long, and out of it I took "Like a Rolling Stone" and made it as a single and I'd never written anything like that before. And it suddenly came to me that that was what I should do.

SONG TITLE **Logical Song**

ARTIST **Supertramp**

Featured on Breakfast in America. Released 1979/A&M
Words & music by Roger Hodgson

Roger Hodgson (singer/songwriter):

You can't preach to people, but you can stimulate their thoughts, and I think that this song does that. I hate to use the word "message," but the thought here is that throughout childhood you are told so many things and yet you are not told anything about your real self. Very rarely anyway. We are taught how to function outwardly but not told who we are inwardly, and no one explains it to us.

SONG TITLE **Love Hurts**

ARTIST **Nazareth**

Featured on Hair of the Dog. Released 1975/A&M
Words & music by Boudleaux Bryant

Don McCafferty (singer/songwriter):

That bloody song has been about and around us for years. We used to play it in pubs when we were all much younger. We'd do it fooling around in the dressing rooms as a warm-up. Then, we heard Emmylou Harris and Gram Parsons do it. We tried it in the studio, and it worked. It opened a lot of American doors for us; it got our name across.

SONG TITLE **Magic Man**

ARTIST Heart

Featured on Dreamboat Annie. Released 1976/Capitol
Words & music by Ann and Nancy Wilson

Ann Wilson (singer/songwriter):

I fell in love with a man, who was Mike Fisher—who didn't want to go to Vietnam. And [he] didn't want to kill people and didn't want to be killed. So we went to Canada and . . . began the band up there with his brother Roger.

Nancy Wilson (singer/songwriter/guitarist):

That's a real reflection of what Ann especially was going through at that time, because she was in love deeply with a guy named Mike Fisher, who was our manager and soundman for live shows. She was really writing the song about when a teenage girl leaves home for the man she loves . . . and how that feels in that leaving-home thing between a girl and her mother. Like throw caution to the wind and follow this guy. It's what she did in real life, she took her guitar and packed a bag and hitchhiked to Vancouver to be with this guy.

SONG TITLE **Mr. Tambourine Man**

ARTIST the Byrds

Featured on Mr. Tambourine Man. Released 1965/Columbia
Words & music by Bob Dylan

Roger McGuinn (singer/songwriter/guitarist):

Terry Melcher [producer] put a Beach Boys kind of track to it. Later in an interview he said that it was "Don't Worry Baby" that he was emulating. And I can kind of hear that, now that I think of it. We cut it down to one verse, and I was shooting for a vocal that was very calculated between John Lennon and Bob Dylan. I was trying to cut some middle ground between those two voices.

SONG TITLE Money

ARTIST Pink Floyd

Featured on Dark Side of the Moon. Released 1973/Capitol
Words & music by Roger Waters

David Gilmour (singer/songwriter/guitarist):

It's Roger's [Waters] riff. Roger came in with the verse and lyrics for "Money" more or less completed. And we just made up middle sections, guitar solos, and all that stuff. We also invented some new riffs—we created a 4/4 progression for the guitar solo and made the poor saxophone player play in 7/4. It was my idea to break down and become dry and empty for the second chorus of the solo.

Alan Parsons (engineer):

A lot of the effects on the album *Dark Side of the Moon* were designed with quad reproduction in mind—most notably the introduction to "Money." The idea was that each part of the cash register would emanate from a different speaker. As a result, lots of time was spent recording each segment of the sound effect on discreet channels. Obviously, no one knew that quad systems would eventually fizzle, but I would say that thinking in quadraphonic terms probably made us more careful about how we recorded the effects.

SONG TITLE **Nights in White Satin**

ARTIST the Moody Blues

Featured on Days of Future Passed. Released 1967/Polydor
Words & music by Justin Hayward

Justin Hayward (singer/songwriter/guitarist):

We were writing and preparing a stage show that was going to be a story about a day in the life of a guy that we used to call the "Moody Blue." . . . I wrote "Nights" as the song that would represent the "night" part of our stage show, and a lot of personal things went into it. Again, it was kind of a risky song, insofar that if you lay your heart bare and leave yourself open, you're game for some incredible criticism; somebody's going to punch you. But ultimately, I think that's what people liked about it.

SONG TITLE **The Pretender**

ARTIST Jackson Browne

Featured on The Pretender. Released 1976/Asylum
Words & music by Jackson Browne

Jackson Browne (singer/songwriter):

For me, "The Pretender" is just the right blend of pessimism and endurance. I mean, for some reason, we go on living, you know. That's such a basic thing. For some reason, there's something in us that makes us keep going: "Now the distance leads me farther on/Though the reasons I once had are gone." The fact is, you probably never even needed a reason to live. What makes these cabdrivers get up every day and go to work? Their lives are probably disgruntled, but they've got this will to live that is really strong. Well, if you weren't like that, you'd check out. A lot of people do, you know. There are statistics, and they're real high. A lot of people kill themselves. But I'm not like that. It's just not part of me to feel that way.

SONG TITLE **Purple Haze**

ARTIST Jimi Hendrix

Featured on Are You Experienced? Released 1967/Reprise
Words & music by Jimi Hendrix

Jimi Hendrix (singer/songwriter/guitarist):

The key to the meaning of the song lies in the line, "That girl put a spell on me," the song just progressed from there. It's got nothing to do with drugs. It's about this guy: this girl turned this cat on and he doesn't know if it's bad or good, that's all, he doesn't know if it's tomorrow or just the end of time, for instance, he likes this girl so much that he doesn't know what he's in, a sort of daze, I suppose. That's what the song is all about.

SONG TITLE **Ridin' the Storm Out**

ARTIST REO Speedwagon

Featured on Ridin' the Storm Out. Released 1973/Epic
Words & music by Gary Richrath

Kevin Cronin (singer/songwriter):

We'd never been to the Rocky Mountains before, we were from Champagne, Illinois. We hit the Colorado border, and there was still flatland and cornfields. And all of a sudden there they were right in front of us—it makes you want to go to the top. We had our ladies with us and we took a couple of bottles of wine, and by the time we had hiked up to the top, there was a big dark storm cloud coming in from the west. So we did what we had to do, we stuck together and kept warm and rode the storm out.

SONG TITLE Roundabout

ARTIST Yes

Featured on Fragile. Released 1972/Atlantic
Words & music by Jon Anderson and Steve Howe

Jon Anderson (singer/songwriter):

We were traveling from Aberdeen through to Glasgow and we'd started this song . . . me and Steve [Howe] were singing it in the back of the van on the way down. One of the things you'll drive through is a very winding small road that goes through this incredible valley and the mountains are sheer from both sides of the road—they just climb to the sky. And because it was a cloudy day, we couldn't see the top of the mountains. We could only see the clouds, because it was sheer straight up . . . I remember saying, "Oh, the mountains—look! They're coming out of the sky!" So we wrote that down: Mountains come out of the sky and they stand there. And we came to a roundabout right at the bottom of this road and within twenty-four hours we were back in London. We'd been on tour then for about a month. So it was sort of twenty-four before I'll be home with my loved one, Jennifer. So the idea was twenty-four before my love and I'll be there with you. In around the lake—just before Glasgow there's a lake—a very famous one—the Loch Ness. So we were driving in around the lake—mountains come out of the sky—they stand there.

Chris Squire (singer/songwriter/bassist):

I don't know if we could ever really do a show without doing "Roundabout," I mean, even though as much as I'd like to not do it!

SONG TITLE Smoke on the Water

ARTIST Deep Purple

Featured on Machine Head. Released 1972/Warner Brothers
Words & music by Ritchie Blackmore, Ian Gillan, Roger Glover, Jon Lord and Ian Paice

Roger Glover (bassist):

We decided to record the album [*Machine Head*] onstage, using the natural acoustics of the surroundings. In other words, make a studio album under live conditions almost like a live album without the audience.

Various places came under consideration, but finally we chose the Casino at Montreux . . . Frank Zappa and the Mothers of Invention were playing an afternoon concert in the Casino the day before we were due to start, and we were invited, and not wishing to confuse our equipment with Zappa's, our roadies decided not to unload that day, but to leave it till the next morning. That decision was possibly the best thing that happened to us in a long time.

The Mothers were roughly two hours into their set when fire broke out. (Later it was discovered that the fire was started by a man with a flare gun, who escaped in the confusion). The music ground to a halt as people started quietly panicking in an orderly fashion. Frank Zappa's parting shot before he fled the stage was "Ah, Arthur Brown in person." Within a few short minutes the place was an inferno. Miraculously nobody was seriously hurt. Claude [Nobs, promoter] worked like a demon organizing the audience out of the building and directing what scanty fire-fighting equipment was available.

It took seven hours to burn itself out. Finally, it became just a smoldering black ruin, leaving a trail of human problems to be sorted out. Claude, of course, suffered a great deal, losing not only a costly amount of hi-fi equipment, but a building whose name had become synonymous with his own, certainly to anyone in the music business. Zappa lost all his equipment—guitars, drums, and encore, and we lost the reason for us being there in the first instance.

Claude, forgetting his own problems, started working to find us a new place. The next day we moved into an old concert hall and started recording that evening.

Ritchie Blackmore (songwriter/guitarist):

We did that track in a different place than the rest of *Machine Head*, which was recorded in the Grand Hotel in Montreux. It was recorded in a big auditorium in Switzerland using the Rolling Stones' mobile studio, which was a truck. For the backing track, we were going for a big, echoey sound. The police started knocking on the door. We knew it was the police, and we knew that they were going to say, "Stop recording!" because they'd had complaints about the noise. So we wouldn't open the door to the police. We asked Martin [Birch], "Is that the one?" And he said, "I don't know. I've got to hear the whole thing all the way through to know if it's the one." The police, who had a fleet of cars outside, kept hammering at the door. We didn't want to open up until we knew we had gotten the right take. Finally, we got it: "No mistakes. That'll do." After that the police said, "You've got to stop. You've got to go somewhere else."

SONG TITLE **Smokin' in the Boy's Room**

ARTIST **Brownsville Station**

Featured on Smokin' in the Boy's Room: The Best of Brownsville Station. Released 1993/Rhino
Words & music by Cub Koda, Michael Lutz

Cub Koda (singer/songwriter):

Me and about five other kids used to smuggle our old man's cigarettes outta the house and head downstairs to the boys' john at the theater. We'd be puffin' on our dads' Old Golds, and the old duffer who owned the theater would come down the steps after us, cursing a blue streak. We'd ditch our butts. He'd be threatening to tell our parents, but he never caught us in the act. When we wrote the tune, I just drew off that experience. It seemed true enough.

SONG TITLE **Sara**

ARTIST **Fleetwood Mac**

Featured on Tusk. Released 1979/Reprise
Words & music by Stevie Nicks

Mick Fleetwood (drummer):

I remember the time when Stevie was writing the song, up at her old house on Doheny. Stevie and Sara would be working, and they'd hear me coming up the drive in my throaty red Ferrari. That's me in the lyric "just like a great dark wing." Stevie brought the song to the studio as a piano track, and I worked for days, sweating bullets to put the time to it. The softness required was a drummer's nightmare, but a great challenge. In the end it took three days to get the brushwork to accompany that piano and vocal. The result was, in many ways, the ultimate Fleetwood Mac song of that era, the late 1970s: breathless, ethereal, almost ecclesiastical and somehow reverent, as Stevie pays tribute to her muse.

SONG TITLE **The Spirit of Radio**

ARTIST Rush

Featured on Permanent Waves. Released 1980/Mercury
Words & music by Alex Lifeson, Geddy Lee and Neil Peart

Alex Lifeson (songwriter/guitarist):

There was a radio station here in Toronto, which is an alternative station now, and that was that station's catch phrase. That song was about the freedom of music and how commercialized radio was becoming. FM radio in the late sixties and early seventies was a bastion of free music, and you got to hear a lot of things that you wouldn't have heard otherwise. It was much like MTV was in the beginning, before it became another big network that feeds a large but very specific segment of the viewing audience. Radio has become a lot more commercialized since then. The station that we wrote that song about won't play our music. As a matter of fact, they played the hell out of the Catherine Wheel's version of that song, but they wouldn't dare play our version.

LED ZEPPELIN: Robert Plant, Jimmy Page,
John Paul Jones, and John Bonham
(Photo by Michael Ochs Archives/Venice, CA)

SONG TITLE Stairway to Heaven

ARTIST Led Zeppelin

Featured on Untitled (Led Zeppelin IV). Released 1971/Atlantic
Words & music by Jimmy Page and Robert Plant

Jimmy Page (songwriter/guitarist):

I'd been fooling around with an acoustic guitar and came up with the different sections which I married together. While I was writing it, I started formulating a few ideas regarding the arrangement. For example, I knew I wanted the drums to rest during the first section. And then after they kicked in, I wanted them to build until we reached a huge crescendo. Also I wanted the tempo to gradually speed up, which is against all musical rules . . . I mean, that's what a musician is not supposed to do, you see?

I had the structure of it, and I ran it by John Paul Jones so he could get the idea; the following day we got into it with John Bonham. Initially, Bonzo couldn't get the timing right on the 12-string part before the solo. You have to realize that at first there was a hell of a lot for everyone to remember on this one. But as we were sort of routining it, Robert was writing down these lyrics, and a huge percentage of the words were written there and then. He didn't have to go away and think about them. Amazing really.

Andy Johns (producer):

I remember saying to Jimmy that I wanted to work on a song that started off real neat and got bigger and bigger and bigger. And Pagey said, "Oh, don't worry, I've got one of those for this album—wait until you hear it!"

John Paul Jones (songwriter/bassist):

I actually like "Stairway." I know that's really corny. But it encompasses a lot of the elements of the band—from the acoustic start to the slightly jazzier section, even, and then to the heavier stuff towards the end. It was a very successful song. I'm not talking about its being successful in commercial terms, but successful in that everything worked well and fell into place. Everything built nicely.

Robert Plant (singer/songwriter):

I truly loathed it. When we used to rehearse, we'd perform "Stairway" as a reggae tune, because Page could never get me to sing it otherwise.

SONG TITLE **Suite: Judy Blue Eyes**

ARTIST Crosby, Stills and Nash

Featured on Crosby, Stills & Nash. Released 1969/Atlantic
Words & music by Stephen Stills

Stephen Stills (singer/songwriter/guitarist):

It started out as a long narrative poem about my relationship with Judy Collins. It poured out of me over many months and filled several notebooks. I had a hell of a time getting the music to fit. I was left with all these pieces of song, and I said, "Let's string them together and call it a suite," because they were all about the same thing and they led up to the same point. And the little kicker at the end about Cuba was just to liven it up because it had gone on forever, and I didn't want it to just fall apart. I said, "Now that we've sung all these lyrics about one thing, let's change the subject entirely." And we did. Even did it in a different language just to make sure that nobody could understand it.

SONG TITLE **Truckin'**

ARTIST **the Grateful Dead**

Featured on American Beauty. Released 1970/Warner Brothers
Words & music by Jerry Garcia, Robert Hunter, Phil Lesh and Bob Weir

Jerry Garcia (singer/songwriter/guitarist):

When Hunter first started writing words for us . . . originally he was on his own trip and he was a poet. He was into the magical thing of words, definitely far out, definitely amazing. The early stuff he wrote that we tried to set to music was stiff because it wasn't really meant to be sung. After he got further and further into it, his craft improved, and then he started going out on the road with us, coming out to see what life was like, to be able to have more of that viewpoint in the music, for the words to be more Grateful Dead words. "Truckin' " is the result of that sort of thing. "Truckin' " is a song we assembled, it didn't . . . it wasn't natural and it didn't flow and it wasn't easy and we really labored over the bastard . . . all of us together.

SONG TITLE **21st Century Schizoid Man**

ARTIST **King Crimson**

Featured on In the Court of the Crimson King. Released 1969/EG
Words & music by Ian McDonald and Pete Sinfield

Ian McDonald (songwriter/instrumentalist):

The riff was written by Greg Lake and myself. This is quite an incredible track—not to everyone's taste perhaps, but definitely innovative. It was well rehearsed and executed, and exciting to record. We deliberately over-gained the vocal on the mixing console and changed the mid-range E.Q. on each hit of the hi-hat on the verses. As I've said before, this track was recorded by all four players from start to finish in one take—almost unheard of these days.

SONG TITLE Walk on the Wild Side

ARTIST Lou Reed

Featured on Transformer. Released 1972/RCA
Words & music by Lou Reed

Lou Reed (singer/songwriter):

If I was to retire now, "Walk on the Wild Side" is the one I'd want to be known by. That's my masterpiece . . . I was supposed to write a play called *Walk on the Wild Side,* and I read the book and wrote the song. Nothing came out of the play, but I wasn't going to waste the time and energy I put into the song.

SONG TITLE You Really Got Me

ARTIST the Kinks

Featured on You Really Got Me. Released 1964/Rhino (rerelease)
Words & music by Ray Davies

Ray Davies (singer/songwriter/guitarist):

I wrote it very quickly: there's just four lines. I thought it was anti all the sweet-sugar songs—"Sweets for My Sweet"—"She Loves You"—which I was rebelling against, maybe because I couldn't write them.

Dave Davies (songwriter/guitarist):

I was never a very good guitarist—so I used to experiment with sounds. I had a little green five watt El Pedo amp with that sort of tinny guitar sound that you'd get. It used to really annoy me, but you couldn't go out and buy amplifiers that didn't sound like that back then. Just out of boredom one day, I slashed the speakers of this little amp with my father's razor.

Ray Davies:

When that record starts, it's like four people doing the four-minute mile. There's a lot of emotion on that record—a lot of determination, fight, and guts in that record.

SONG TITLE Your Song

ARTIST Elton John

Featured on Elton John. Released 1970/MCA
Words & music by Elton John and Bernie Taupin

Elton John (singer/songwriter/pianist):

"Your Song" you just can't get away from. It is a beautiful song. It's lyrically beautiful. It was written in about five minutes, recorded in two.

Bernie Taupin (lyricist):

It's the song you hear everywhere, you hear it at Safeway, you hear it at Ralph's, you hear it in the elevator in the Holiday Inn, you hear it in the piano bar in the Holiday Inn—you hear it all over the Holiday Inn . . . . It's become a Holiday Inn song.

The 25 Classic Rock Albums of All Time

1

The Beatles—Sgt. Pepper's Lonely Hearts Club Band

Classic Rock Songs: Sgt. Pepper/With a Little Help from My Friends, Lucy in the Sky with Diamonds, A Day in the Life.

• *Sgt. Pepper* represents a milestone in popular music. It is the peak of the Beatles' recorded output, representing their last truly collaborative effort. *Sgt. Pepper* was also one of the first albums conceived as a complete listening experience. Previously popular albums were generally a couple of hit singles patched together with some album tracks and some filler to create the necessary minutes for two LP sides. The Beatles changed all of that forever by releasing this very psychedelic work at the peak of the summer of love, influencing hundreds of up-and-coming musicians.

The four meticulous months spent putting the album together were like an aural experiment in a sonic laboratory. The Beatles used the studio as an instrument: changing tape speeds, experimenting with microphone placement, using unconventional instruments, flirting with different styles of music, etc. The project was to be a song cycle based on the Beatles' lives starting with "Strawberry Fields Forever" and "Penny Lane." However, the recording process became expensive and behind schedule, so the two songs were released as a single and the song cycle was dropped. The "Lonely Hearts" concept joined the individual songs together to form a cohesive package.

2

Pink Floyd—Dark Side of the Moon

Classic Rock Songs: Money, Time, Us and Them.

• It is fascinating that an album whose central theme is madness would become one of the most consistently popular albums of all time. From an audiophile's standpoint this record is a follow-up to *Sgt. Pepper* with its wide variety of sound effects (heartbeats, clocks, and cash registers chiming, people muttering, etc.) and studio trickery. In fact, this album was used to demonstrate high-quality stereo systems for many years. *Dark Side* represents the pinnacle of Pink Floyd; although their following albums were artistic and commercial successes, they progressively became solo projects for singer/songwriter Roger Waters. The unmistakable "Floydian" sound is captured in all its glory on this LP: the use of hypnotic slow tempos, the lush textures of the instruments, the gorgeous guitar and saxophone solos, and the dark lyrical vision courtesy of Mr. Waters. *Dark Side of the Moon* was enormously successful (it is the fourth-best selling album of all time, and it managed to stay on the *Billboard* charts for an unprecedented 736 weeks!) and its continued popularity is a bit of a mystery even to the band members themselves. As their drummer Nick Mason has said, "Everyone thought it was the best thing we'd done to date, and everyone was very pleased with it. But there's no way that anyone felt it was five times as good as *Meddle* or eight times as good as *Atom Heart Mother*—the sort of figures it, in fact, sold."

3

The Rolling Stones—Let It Bleed

Classic Rock Songs: Gimme Shelter, Midnight Rambler, You Can't Always Get What You Want

• A true classic that captures the Stones in their prime and at the height of their creative powers. *Let It Bleed* contained tremendous songwriting that would never be equalled by the band. It was recorded at a crucial juncture in the band's history, when Brian Jones, the Rolling Stones' founding guitarist, was kicked out of the group for his excessive drug use. After a series of auditions, Mick Taylor of the Bluesbreakers (Eric Clapton's replacement in that band) was chosen to take his place. After *Let It Bleed*'s release it attained the legendary FM radio status that most bands can only dream about.

4

The Jimi Hendrix Experience—Are You Experienced?

Classic Rock Songs: Purple Haze, Are You Experienced?, Foxey Lady, Manic Depression, The Wind Cries Mary

• If Jimi Hendrix hadn't been born, someone would have had to invent him. Truly the electric guitar as an instrument was transformed in his hands. Hendrix managed to break through the barrier between innovation and enormous commercial success. Certainly any rock guitarist today owes him a debt of gratitude. His first album was one of his best and most influential, containing many of his classic songs and performances.

5

The Who—Who's Next

Classic Rock Songs: Baba O'Riley, Won't Get Fooled Again, Behind Blue Eyes

• After the Who's huge success with their rock opera *Tommy*, they committed themselves to making an ambitious follow-up entitled *Lifehouse*. Peter Townshend crafted the piece carefully, infusing it with some of his finest work. Unfortunately, the work proved to be too unwieldy and complex, and the band was left at a crucial crossroads. The solution was to call in a new producer and rerecord some material along with salvaging songs from the *Lifehouse* project. The band members weren't overjoyed with the result, but felt at least the ordeal was over. The resulting album was one of their finest, featuring the band in their prime playing timeless material such as "Baba O'Riley" (so named after Indian spiritual master Maher Baba and composer Terry Riley) and "Won't Get Fooled Again."

6

Led Zeppelin—Untitled

Classic Rock Songs: Rock & Roll, Black Dog, Stairway to Heaven

• After the mixed critical response to *Led Zeppelin III,* the band quietly rented a mobile unit to record their new album. There was an immediacy to its sound and certain tracks like "Rock & Roll" were basically cut live as they were created. As the LP progressed, it was clear that they had come up with their most diverse work—a real combination of the soft acoustic numbers and the all-out rockers. And of course there was a song called "Stairway to Heaven" that combined these elements to create the definitive Led Zeppelin classic. To remove themselves from the hype that surrounded some of their previous releases, the band decided to leave the album untitled (except for the quasi-mystical symbols on the inner sleeve) and keep the name of the band off the record's artwork. Despite the strong protests of their record company, who believed this move was commercial suicide, the band argued that "the music is more important" and won out. Needless to say, Led Zeppelin fans were indeed able to deduce who created this music.

7

Fleetwood Mac—Rumours

Classic Rock Songs: The Chain, Dreams, Gold Dust Woman, Go Your Own Way

• This album proves true the concept that sometimes conflict in a creative relationship is inspiring. Fleetwood Mac's personnel were reeling from three broken relationships at the recording of *Rumours* (two of them were inter-band: Steve Nicks/Lindsey Buckingham, Christine McVie/John McVie) and incredibly, by channeling that energy into the music, they made their finest album. As Mick Fleetwood recalls, "[It would] take us almost a year, during which we spoke to each other in clipped, civil tones while sitting in small, airless studios listening to each other's songs about our own shattered relationships." Also enormous amounts of cocaine were consumed by musicians and engineers, destroying their perspective and slowing the work to a snail's pace. However, the resulting breakup songs were worth the wait. The crystalline production and flawless performance can still be heard on any rock FM radio station.

8

Crosby, Stills, Nash, and Young—*Déjà Vu*

Classic Rock Songs: Carry On, Teach Your Children, Our House, Woodstock

• Whereas their first album had come together relatively easily, Crosby, Stills, Nash (and now Young) had a very difficult time recording *Déjà Vu.* It seemed that everyone was having emotional and relationship problems, and to top it off the egos that had been submerged previously had come out in full force. Perfectionist tendencies kept the group reworking material endlessly, until some frustrated members had given up hope that the record would see the light of day. When it was released, fans were treated to the band's strongest, most consistent set yet. These many years later they have yet to follow it up with material and performances as powerful.

9

The Eagles—*Hotel California*

Classic Rock Songs: Hotel California, New Kid in Town, Life in the Fast Lane

• This classic album by the Eagles was by all accounts an ordeal to create. The band went into the studio with very little material prepared and watched the studio hours tick by as they struggled to come up with the music, arrangements, and lyrics. It was a tortuously long process with Don Henley and Glenn Frey acting as dictators over the ensemble. They were known to nitpick over every detail in a song, sometimes spending days getting a chorus just right. This zealous quest for perfection paid off, but as Bob Seger said later it would cost the group its life.

10

The Doors—The Doors

Classic Rock Songs: Light My Fire, Break on Through (To the Other Side), The End

• This remains an exciting and innovative debut album from the Doors. They pushed the envelope with both lyrical and musical content on many of the songs. It was recorded in six days by capturing their live act on tape. The single "Light My Fire" was a number one single and brought the band enormous success. The album contained other songs that received considerable airplay: "Break on Through (To the Other Side)," "Twentieth Century Fox" and "The End." The songs firmly cemented the Doors' sound, with its organ/guitar (no bass!) combinations and Jim Morrison's dramatic baritone vocals, as a classic rock staple.

11

Elton John—Goodbye Yellow Brick Road

Classic Rock Songs: Goodbye Yellow Brick Road, Candle in the Wind, Saturday Night's Alright for Fighting, Funeral for a Friend/Love Lies Bleeding

• One of the amazing things about this perennially popular Elton John album was the speed in which it was written and recorded (and Elton was known for his ability to put out two quality albums a year in the seventies). He decided that the time had come to record at a new locale, so the band, with producer Gus Dudgeon, headed out to Jamaica to lay down tracks. When they arrived to find a decidedly inferior recording studio, Elton retreated to his hotel room armed with new Bernie Taupin lyrics and began writing new songs. By the time the band decided to return to Europe to record the LP properly, they had enough material for a consistently strong double album. *Goodbye Yellow Brick Road* was recorded in a mere 12 days and is considered the high watermark of Elton's reign of popularity.

12

Steely Dan—Pretzel Logic

Classic Rock Songs: Rikki Don't Lose That Number, Pretzel Logic, Any Major Dude Will Tell You

• This album marks the end of Steely Dan the band and signifies the beginning of Steely Dan the studio collective. Songwriters Donald Fagen and Walter Becker began to assume control of the operation and started calling in the cream of L.A.'s studio musicians to record Pretzel Logic, using band members only for occasional overdubs. It was an arduous process, but the resulting album was worth the effort. It featured the gorgeous (and most successful single) "Rikki Don't Lose That Number" and many of the other tunes that earned them their reputation as the best songwriters of the time. Certainly the critics loved it and were spouting things like *Downbeat* magazine's review, "there are no better rock recording groups in America, and damn few worldwide."

13

The Moody Blues—Days of Future Passed

Classic Rock Songs: Nights in White Satin, Tuesday Afternoon

• This album was created out of deceit. The Moodies were dealing with the relative failure of their R & B career and had decided to shift styles. They hired new band members to give the band an infusion of new songwriting talent and began writing material with a "cosmic" edge to it. A record company approached them to record a rock version of Dvořák's *New World Symphony* with the London Festival Orchestra. They agreed to this idea, but when they got into the studio, they began recording their own material. The result was probably the most successful integration of orchestra and rock band and became the Moodies first gold album. This album has had renewed interest and popularity over the years, reaching number 3 on the American charts four years after its initial release.

Jethro Tull—Aqualung

Classic Rock Songs: Aqualung, Cross-Eyed Mary, Locomotive Breath, My God

• By 1972 Jethro Tull was starting to break all over the world. Their previous LP *Benefit* had done excellent business around the world, and they settled in Island studios to record the follow-up. Unfortunately, the studio was new and fraught with technical difficulties. The sessions were frustrating and the thoroughly demoralized group members felt they had failed to do the material justice with the inferior production. They did as much as they could in the mixing and post-production to make the record presentable and hoped for the best as they went on tour. Remarkably, they were more than able to salvage the work for *Aqualung*, and it has become one of the strongest albums of their career. Ian Anderson's thematic work (it was not really a "concept" album) about man and religion touched listeners, perhaps because as one reviewer said, "He wants to make us *think!*"

15

David Bowie—The Rise and Fall of Ziggy Stardust and the Spiders from Mars

Classic Rock Songs: Ziggy Stardust, Suffragette City

• This is an excellent concept album, illustrating Bowie's idea of a plastic rock star, Ziggy Stardust. His lyrical vision, coupled with music drawn from many different styles and influences, created an unforgettable listening experience. Lead guitarist Mick Ronson's playing is prominently featured on many of these songs to good effect. With this record, Bowie became identified as Ziggy Stardust (whom he portrayed as an actor in concert). This move brought him notoriety and success, but became a hindrance once it became difficult to disassociate himself from his creation.

16

Cream—*Disraeli Gears*

Classic Rock Songs: Sunshine of Your Love, Strange Brew

• This album would be indispensable just for "Sunshine of Your Love," a guitar-heavy classic rock staple (Eric Clapton later said that its guitar riff was a dedication to Jimi Hendrix). In contrast to the first record (which was issued only six months before), *Disraeli Gears* did not cover blues songs, and the band members began writing material of their own. Their exploration of drugs, psychedelia, and heavy metal on this album had a profound impact on their peers (as well as a new generation of up-and-coming musicians).

17

Peter Frampton—*Frampton Comes Alive!*

Classic Rock Songs: Show Me the Way; Baby, I Love Your Way; Do You Feel Like We Do?

• This live album represents a summation of Peter Frampton's career up to that point. He had released four studio albums that had done reasonable business, but for some reason had a much larger live audience. He decided it was time to capture his band live, performing the cream of his material thinking it might sell 500,000 pieces. He was off by just a little bit—*Frampton Comes Alive!* became one of the best-selling albums of all time. The recording has the spontaneity and power of rock music that hasn't been retouched in the studio. As

Frampton has said, "Throughout *Comes Alive* there are a lot of places where I go, 'Ohh!' But the feel is there. I don't sing in tune the whole way. My guitar goes a little sharp sometimes or flat. The bass might be out of tune." The body of the album was recorded in three different shows in San Francisco to make a single record. But when Jerry Moss (the "M" in A&M Records) heard the mixes for the album, he told the band that they were missing important songs and that it had to be a double. So Frampton had his band do five or six more shows to fill out the album.

18

Lynyrd Skynyrd—(pronounced leh-nerd skin-nerd)

Classic Rock Songs: Free Bird, Simple Man, Gimmie Three Steps, Tuesday's Gone

• This album is a perfect introduction to Southern rock music. Many of these songs are considered to be classics and get regular airplay on FM radio. The album features the powerful guitar work of Allen Collins, Gary Rossington, and Ed King as well as lead singer Ronnie Van Zant's upfront vocals. The song "Free Bird" is still one of the most requested songs on the radio.

19

Boston—Boston

Classic Rock Songs: More than a Feeling, Peace of Mind, Foreplay/Long Time

• This is one of the best-selling debut albums of all time (with over nine million copies sold). Tom Scholz was known to take years to perfect an album, and that certainly paid off handsomely on this package. Amazingly, most of the album was recorded and mixed in his basement studio. The songwriting was very strong and the playing was good, but it was the production that was the star. It was so clean it practically had a sheen to it, and was the perfect setting for Boston's multitracked vocal harmonies (courtesy of Brad Delp) and Scholz's inspired guitar work.

20

Yes—Fragile

Classic Rock Songs: Roundabout, Long Distance Runaround, Heart of the Sunrise

• After an American tour and just before the sessions started for this album, Yes keyboardist Tony Kaye was let go for personal and professional reasons. The very talented Rick Wakeman took his place, and the record was made in just a few short weeks. *Fragile* was originally a double album, with one LP of studio recordings and the other a live disk, but Yes dropped that idea because of the time they needed to put it together. In addition to the four major compositions on this record, Yes decided that each band member would have the opportunity to showcase his talents on an individual solo track. This album also marked the first of many successful collaborations between Yes and the artist Roger Dean. Their music and his exotic, surreal landscapes became irrevocably associated with each other over the years. The band toured incessantly after *Fragile* came out and for the first time were a major headlining act.

21

Aerosmith—Toys in the Attic

Classic Rock Songs: Sweet Emotion, Walk This Way, Toys in the Attic, Big Ten Inch Record

• Although this was Aerosmith's third record, it was the first to really capture the intensity of their live performances. The band was fueled on by various illegal substances and committed some of their best songs to tape. As bassist Tom Hamilton explains, "We really did put everything we had into that record, and I guess the reason it turned out so well was because we had the perfect combination of great songs and the kind of 'fired up' spirit that you get after a lot of touring."

22

The Byrds—Byrds' Greatest Hits

Classic Rock Songs: Turn! Turn! Turn!, Eight Miles High, Mr. Tambourine Man

• The title says it all, doesn't it? The Byrds were extremely influential in the burgeoning folk-rock movement in the mid-sixties. Songs such as "Turn! Turn! Turn!", "Eight Miles High," and "Mr. Tambourine Man" were all huge hits and had an enormous impact on people like Tom Petty, REM, and the Eagles.

23

Queen—A Night at the Opera

Classic Rock Songs: Bohemian Rhapsody, You're My Best Friend, Death on Two Legs

• The careful attention to detail and extremely meticulous work of Queen and producer Roy Thomas Baker on *Night at the Opera* did not go unnoticed by the world. The Queen sound by definition was filled with electric guitars in harmony, a rock-solid rhythm section, and many layers of vocals. The group was a little concerned that the lead-off single "Bohemian Rhapsody" was a bit over the top; it would either be a huge success or an equally huge failure. This strange song with suicidal overtones, mood changes, and a pseudo-operatic section was incredibly well received all over the world. Its popularity encouraged the band to be even more outrageous. However, this record is much more than "Bohemian Rhapsody," and it remains the most consistently entertaining album in their history.

24

AC/DC—Back in Black

Classic Rock Songs: Back in Black, You Shook Me

• It doesn't get any simpler than this meat-and-potatoes rock and roll. AC/DC was never a band to bother with any niceties in their music, with completely straight-ahead guitar power chords, brutal beats pounded out in 4/4 time, and blistering vocals on top. The group had quite a worldwide following when they were faced with the loss of their original singer Bon Scott, who drank himself to death. The group survived and found a suitable replacement in vocalist Brian Johnson. The resulting album was in part a tribute to their fallen comrade in arms.

25

Deep Purple—Machine Head

Classic Rock Songs: Smoke on the Water, Highway Star, Space Truckin'

• Deep Purple had been slightly dissatisfied with their studio sound on their previous album and decided to try and get a more "live" sound and feel for their next project. They went to Montreux to record *Machine Head* (as documented on page 170) and emerged with the finest music of their career. The songwriting was extremely strong, and the performances were incendiary (particularly the work of guitarist Ritchie Blackmore and organist Jon Lord). *Machine Head* firmly established the group as a heavy metal giant and even challenged Led Zeppelin with its success.

Jurassic Park

Are your favorite dinosaurs walking the earth?

AC/DC—The group has continued to play its own brand of hard rock to slightly smaller crowds over the years. Their latest album is the delightfully titled *Ballbreaker*, which followed the live recording, imaginatively titled *AC/DC Live*.

The Allman Brothers Band—The group broke up two times (once in 1975 and then again in 1981) before regrouping in 1989. Since then they have replaced departed members with a revolving turnstile of musicians.

Bad Company—Bad Company called it quits by 1983, but by the late 1980s original members Mick Ralphs and Simon Kirke brought in new members to re-create the band. Unfortunately, their distinctive vocalist Paul Rodgers did not return, and the new lineup created music that was anonymous at best.

Badfinger—The story of this talented band is marred by tragedy. After a dispute about money, their record company pulled their then current release from the market. This, and other personal reasons, prompted Pete Ham (guitar/vocals) to commit suicide by hanging himself in his garage. In the late seventies the band tried to re-form and released a couple of minor albums. Frustrated by the business, Tom Evans (bass/vocals) took his life in 1983. Only member Joey Molland has continued occasionally touring under the Badfinger name (with other sidemen filling out the band).

The Band—After playing what was supposed to be their last gig in Winterland on Thanksgiving 1976 (later documented on the film and album

The Last Waltz) Robbie Robertson (songwriter) left the band. One of their keyboardists, Richard Manuel, committed suicide, but the Band decided to regroup without these two members and to go on the road again. They also recorded a fine album in 1993 entitled *Jericho* that was their best effort in many years.

Pat Benatar—Pat Benatar's commercial slide began with the 1984 album *Tropico*, where she had changed her musical direction to be more mainstream (as opposed to her brand of melodic hard rock). She continued to embrace different styles (including the blues) before going back to rock. She has toured and released albums to varying interest.

Black Sabbath—After Ozzy Osbourne left in 1979 the other members also gradually departed, until guitarist Tony Iommi was the only original band member remaining. He continued to reinvent the band with new members to less and less musical and commercial success. Their one-off performance at Live Aid inspired the band to reunite the first lineup of Black Sabbath, but this idea wasn't realized until 1997 on Ozzy's tour.

Blue Oyster Cult—The public started deserting BOC, and changes to the band roster and sporadic, uneven albums didn't help matters. BOC remains at this time in limbo.

David Bowie—David Bowie decided late in his career to get a fresh start. He informed the public that he would no longer be performing his old classics in concert and started a new band called Tin Machine. Their two albums were remarkably unsuccessful, and Bowie returned to his solo career.

Chicago—The band was in serious trouble after the accidental death of guitarist Terry Kath (from a handgun). They were able to regroup and produce some very successful albums in the early eighties before their lead singer Peter Cetera left to start a solo career. They have had some hits since then, but have suffered from diminishing returns.

Eric Clapton—Clapton's career was on a decidedly downward turn in the mid-eighties. He was releasing albums on a regular basis to smaller and smaller audiences. It wasn't until his enormously popular *Unplugged* album in 1992 that his career was completely revived. Its appeal lay in the fact that Eric had forsook the polished, slick sound of his studio recordings to do what he does the best—play the blues.

Creedence Clearwater Revival—After John Fogerty left the band in the late seventies, the remaining members amazingly decided to continue on (under a different name, yet utilizing the CCR connection in their advertising).

Deep Purple—Purple reunited in the mid-eighties after being on ice for several years. Their initial comeback record *Perfect Strangers* did excellent business and gave the band momentum for several years. Recently guitarist Ritchie Blackmore was replaced by Steve Morse (Dregs, Kansas).

The Doobie Brothers—After their breakup in 1981 the members of the Doobie Brothers went on to solo careers, with Michael McDonald enjoying the most popularity. The early lineup of the band (without McDonald) reunited in 1987 and has been touring and recording ever since.

Eagles—After the release of their live album, they broke up to start solo careers (with uneven degrees of success). In 1994 they re-formed to find thousands of eager fans willing to support their appropriately titled *Hell Freezes Over* album and tour.

ELO—Amazingly, after the band folded, Bev Bevan (the drummer!) decided to reform the group without singer/songwriter Jeff Lynne or any other original member. Because of legal reasons he was forced to call this outfit ELO II.

Emerson, Lake and Palmer—In 1980, after the completion of the horrible *Love Beach* record, the band dissolved. They participated in various regroupings (such as Three, and Emerson Lake Powell) before coming together to create *Black Moon*. The following work—*In the Hot Seat*—was a complete disaster. In the summer of 1996 ELP regrouped and completed an excellent double bill with Jethro Tull.

Fleetwood Mac—After Lindsey Buckingham split in 1987, the group soldiered on. They produced some lackluster work before Stevie Nicks and Christine McVie also decided to go solo. Fleetwood Mac was reunited in 1997 for the very successful *The Dance* album and tour.

Foreigner—Singer Lou Gramm left in the late '80s for a solo career, and the band unfortunately chose to continue with a new singer. The fans did notice and stayed away in droves. Recently Gramm and the band were together again touring and releasing music.

Genesis—Until recently this band was more successful with each release. A small sampling of their hits include "Turn It On Again," "Abacab," "That's All," "Invisible Touch," "I Can't Dance." In 1997 singer Phil Collins left the band for his solo career and remaining members Tony Banks and Mike Rutherford replaced him with Ray Wilson. The resulting album—*Calling All Stations*—was released in September of 1997 with nowhere near the high profile and interest garnered by earlier albums. A tour of North America was scheduled, then postponed until the summer of 1998.

George Harrison—After releasing the horrible *Gone Troppo* in 1982 Harrison took an extended break. He came back with *Cloud Nine*, an excellent record (perhaps his best since *All Things Must Pass*). Since then he has put out a live record and had a hand in the archival Beatles Anthology project.

Heart—The members of Heart dwindled down to the core of Ann and Nancy Wilson and Howard Lesse. They continue to release sporadic albums with the latest being 1993's *Desire Walks On*.

Jethro Tull—Singer Ian Anderson and guitarist Martin Barre have formed the permanent nucleus of the band and have watched a parade of musicians fill the various positions. The album *Crest of a Knave* met with critical and commercial success and Jethro Tull has intermittently released albums since that time. Their tours are well attended by their loyal following and Tull's current album is entitled *Roots to Branches*.

Elton John—By the end of 1976 Elton's luck had changed considerably. He had basically ruled the charts in the seventies, but now he had run out of steam. Elton took an extended vacation, and for the first time worked apart from his songwriting partner Bernie Taupin. The solo albums produced in the eighties had sold less than albums released at his peak, but still did respectable business. Elton revitalized his career in the '90s by writing the music for the *Lion King* and performing at Princess Diana's funeral.

Journey—Journey disbanded in 1987 with members Neal Schon and Jonathan Cain forming Bad English and singer Steve Perry continuing his solo career. They all got back together for the platinum selling album *Trial By Fire*. Interestingly, the band did not follow up with a tour. Some say Steve Perry was injured in an accident on the Hawaiian Islands, but the band's failure to tour may be that the band members just can't get along.

Kiss—After appearing on MTV's unplugged with original members Peter Criss and Ace Frehley, Kiss decided to regroup for a tour. All of the costumes, makeup, and special effects were trotted out to create the ultimate Kiss show. It was wildly popular and became one of the best-selling tours of the year.

Led Zeppelin—With the death of drummer John Bonham, Led Zeppelin ceased to exist. The remaining members worked on solo projects with varying degrees of success until recently when Jimmy Page and Robert Plant rejoined forces to create the *No Quarter* album and tour.

John Lennon—After leaving the Beatles he released several experimental albums in collaboration with his wife Yoko Ono. In the early seventies he produced what is considered his finest work—*Plastic Ono Band* and *Imagine*. His following albums were not as artistically or commercially successful, and by 1976 he retired for five years to raise his son Sean. In 1980 he ended his retirement with the creation of his record *Double Fantasy*. He was killed by an assassin's bullet outside of his home in New York on December 8, 1980.

Lynyrd Skynyrd—Unfortunately, a plane crash in 1977 put an end to Skynyrd at the height of its popularity. Various members formed groups like the Rossington-Collins Band, but finally the remaining members came together for a tribute tour in 1987. This proved to be so popular that the band stayed together to create more albums and to continue touring.

Paul McCartney—After the Beatles split up, Paul McCartney had the most success as a solo act. He and his band Wings scored with numerous hit singles and albums. This trend slowed down noticeably in the '80s and '90s, but after the Beatles Anthology series came out, Paul released his most popular album in years, *Flaming Pie*.

Steve Miller—Has never stopped recording and touring. His latest album is the box set that was released in 1994.

The Moody Blues—After a five-year break the Moodies re-formed to create the album *Octave* (after which their keyboardist Mike Pinder left). His replacement, Patrick Moraz, joined for the resulting tour, and the following record *Long Distance Voyager* was a huge hit. They have continued to release albums and tour on a regular basis.

Pink Floyd—The band re-formed (minus singer/songwriter Roger Waters) to create two best-selling studio albums and two live albums. Their latest is *Pulse*, a document of their last tour (the album features a complete performance of *Dark Side of the Moon*).

Queen—Unfortunately, Queen disbanded after lead singer Freddie Mercury's death from AIDS, (but who on earth could replace him?). A special tribute concert was organized with predictably mixed results, and the remaining members have put out several posthumous albums.

REO Speedwagon—REO Speedwagon continues to play the theater markets throughout the United States. Their latest is entitled *Building the Bridge* (which President Clinton appropriated for his purposes).

The Rolling Stones—Like some kind of force of nature, the Stones never go away, and every few years or so an album and a tour come out for the world to see. The latest is the *Bridges to Babylon* extravaganza.

Rush—Rush continues to be a three-man operation. They are an abnormality in that they have never broken up and soldier on with the same lineup (Neil Peart, the newest member, joined the band for its second album).

Santana—Carlos Santana has never stopped playing with fire and passion. His most recent release is a box set *(Dance of the Rainbow Serpent)*, covering his fine catalog over the years.

Bob Seger—Seger has never lost his audience or appeal in live performances. His 1996 tour was one of the top-ten grossing tours of the year.

Bruce Springsteen—Bruce gave the E St. Band their walking papers after the *Tunnel of Love* tour. His latest release is the low-key *The Ghost of Tom Joad* (a musical interpretation of *The Grapes of Wrath*). He featured the album on an intimate tour of small theaters.

Steely Dan—The popular duo of Donald Fagen and Walter Becker broke up after the release of their album *Gaucho.* However, they have continued to assist each other in the production of the other's solo albums and more recently put together a touring version of Steely Dan.

Rod Stewart—Rod has promised to keep singing until he drops, and it looks like he will keep his promise. He has a solid fan base that turns out for the shows and buys all of the albums (the most recent is *If We Fell in Love Tonight*).

Supertramp—The group split up after the lackluster sales of *Free as a Bird.* The solo careers of the band members floundered until they recently reunited (without longtime singer/songwriter Roger Hodgson).

The Who—Artistically even Pete Townshend admits the Who was spent after 1972. However, even the death of drummer Keith Moon didn't stop the band from releasing mediocre album after album. After the appropriately titled *It's Hard* came out and was promoted on tour, the band broke up. A series of compilations to milk the consumers' dollars followed (they have more "Best of"/"Live" collections then they do actual studio albums!) and later there were reunions to promote stage productions of *Tommy* and *Quadrophenia.*

Yes—By 1980 the classic lineup had broken up due to financial and personality difficulties. However, they re-formed with the addition of guitarist Trevor Rabin to create their most successful album, *90125*, with the number one hit single "Owner of a Lonely Heart." Their next record, *Big Generator*, was not as successful, and lead singer Jon Anderson formed a rival Yes band featuring other former band members and called it Anderson Bruford Wakeman Howe. This group put out an album and went on tour before reuniting with the remaining members to form an eight-man super Yes. Since 1994 the band has gone through several personnel changes, but as of this writing they have released two double live albums entitled *Keys to Ascension* and *Keys to Ascension II*.

Neil Young—Amazingly Neil Young has become an icon to the alternative crowd (like some sort of grunge godfather). He is held in such esteem for appearing to not sell out; he has been at odds many times with his record companies, who have felt that his product was commercial suicide.

ZZ Top—ZZ Top has never stopped chugging along. Their brand of synthesized blues is not quite as popular as it has been in years past, but these guys seem to ignore the sales and get out on the road and play.

Sources

I am gratefully indebted to the sources below for material used in this book.

Books

AC/DC by Martin Huxley
Aerosmith by Martin Huxley
Bachman-Turner Overdrive by Martin Melhuish
The Band by Barney Hoskyns
Behind the Hits by Bob Shannon/John Jama
Between the Lines [Lou Reed] by Michael Wream
Billboard Number #1 Albums by Craig Rosen
The Billboard Book of #1 Hits by Fred Bronson
The Book of Genesis by Hugh Fielder
The British Invasion by Nicholas Schaffner
Bowie by Jerry Hopkins
CSN: The Authorized Biography by Dave Zimmer
Cult Rockers by Wayne Janick/Tad Lathrop
Don't You Want Somebody to Love? [Jefferson Airplane] by Darby Slick
Down Thunder Road by Marc Eliot
Bob Dylan: In His Own Words by Barry Miles
The Encyclopedia of Pop, Rock and Soul by Irwin Stambler
Fleetwood by Mick Fleetwood/Stephen Davis
Genesis—I Know What I Like by Armando Gallo
I Me Mine by George Harrison/Derek Taylor
Janis by David Dalton
Elton John by Philip Norman
Elton John Tapes by Andy Peebles

The Kinks by Jon Savage
The Kinks Kronikles by John Medelssohn
Led Zeppelin: The Press Reports by Robert Godwin
Lennon by Ray Coleman
Life in the Fast Lane [Aerosmith] by Malcolm Doom
Long Time Gone [David Crosby] by David Crosby/Carl Gottlieb
Magic Carpet Ride [Steppenwolf] by John Kay and John Einarson
The Making of Led Zeppelin's (fourth album) by Robert Godwin
Jim Morrison—Dark Star by Dylan Jones
No One Gets Out of Here Alive by Jerry Hopkins/Danny Sugerman
The Penguin Book of Rock and Roll Writing by Clinton Heylin
Pink Floyd—A Visual Documentary by Miles Mabbett
Pink Floyd—Wish You Were Here Song Book
Queen by Stephen Rider
Keith Richards: The Biography by Victor Bockris
Rock World—As Bold As Love by Eddie Brigati
Rock Lives by Timothy White
The Rolling Stone Interviews, by the editors of *RS*
Linda Ronstadt—Rock Star by Mark Bego
Seeds of Change by Kenneth Boa and Kerry Livgren
She Bop by Lucy O'Brien
Songwriters on Songwriting by Paul Zollo
Bruce Springsteen in His Own Words by John Duffy
Rod Stewart—Vagabond Heart by Geoffrey Giuliano
The Supertramp Book by Martin Melhuish
What's That Sound? [Elton John] by Ben Fong-Torres
The Who: In Their Own Words by Steve Clarke
Wouldn't It Be Nice? by Brian Wilson/Todd Gold
Written in My Soul by Bill Flanagan
Neil Young in His Own Words by Michael Heatley
Neil Young: The Man and His Music by David Downing
Neil Young: The Rolling Stone Files by the editors of *Rolling Stone*
The Frank Zappa Companion by Richard Kostelanetz/John Rocco

Magazines

BAM
Circus

Creem
Guitar for the Practicing Musician
November 1992, George Harrison Gets Back by Vic Garbarini
Guitar Legends
Guitar Player
The Billy Gibbons Interview, February 1981
The Tom Petty Interview, August 1986
The Eric Clapton Interview, August 1976
The Keith Richards Interview, November 1977
Guitar School
Guitar World
Keyboard
The Keith Emerson Interview, October 1977
Musician
Playboy
Progression
Rolling Stone
"Stevie Nicks' Magic Act" by Timothy White, Sept. 3, 1981
"Fortunate Son" by Michael Goldberg, Feb. 4, 1993
"Eric Clapton: In His Own Words" April 29, 1993
"Jagger Remembers" by Jann Wenner, Dec. 14, 1995

Radio Shows and Special Edition Albums

CSN Box Set
Jimi Hendrix: *Are You Experienced?*
Jethro Tull: *Aqualung*
Kansas Box Set
Neil Young—*Decade*
In the Studio:
Yes—*Fragile*
Kansas—*Leftoverture*
Kansas—*Point of Know Return*
Journey—*Infinity*
Bad Company—*Bad Company*
Pat Benatar—*Crimes of Passion*
The Source with Charlie K.
"The Wall" The BBC with Tom Vance

Videos

The Moody Blues—*Legend of a Band*
Elton John—*Two Rooms*
The Doobie Brothers—*Listen to the Music*
Foreigner—*Feels Like the Very First Time*
The Who's *Tommy—The Amazing Journey*
The Band—*The Authorized Video Biography*
Journey—*Frontiers & Beyond*

Song Index